★★★★★★★★★★ WHAT ★★★★★★★★★★
WASHINGTON
CAN LEARN FROM THE
WORLD OF SPORTS

★★★★★★★★★★★ WHAT ★★★★★★★★★★★★
WASHINGTON
CAN LEARN FROM THE
WORLD OF SPORTS

FOREWORD BY "DEACON" JONES ★ AFTERWORD BY J.C. WATTS

GEORGE ALLEN

FORMER GOVERNOR OF VIRGINIA AND UNITED STATES SENATOR

Since 1947
REGNERY
PUBLISHING, INC.
An Eagle Publishing Company • Washington, DC

Cataloging-in-Publication data on file with the Library of Congress

ISBN 978-1-59698-598-8

Published in the United States by
Regnery Publishing, Inc.
One Massachusetts Avenue, NW
Washington, DC 20001

www.regnery.com

Manufactured in the United States of America

10 9 8 7 6 5 4 3 2 1

Books are available in quantity for promotional or premium use. Write to Director of Special Sales, Regnery Publishing, Inc., One Massachusetts Avenue NW, Washington, DC 20001, for information on discounts and terms or call (202) 216-0600.

Distributed to the trade by:
Perseus Distribution
387 Park Avenue South
New York, NY 10016

Dedicated to the invigorating memory of my father,
Coach Allen, and my still kicking, vivacious mother, Etty.

And to my loyal, coaching wife Susan and our children:
thoughtful Tyler, gentleman Forrest, and energetic Brooke.

TABLE OF CONTENTS

What Washington Can Learn from the World of Sports is a must read for all citizens of this democracy. As you read this book, you will understand why Senator Allen is saying that politics need to have the character of sports. We must come together as a team to solve the pressing problems that face us all. Sports is all about winning the game, winning in life and winning in business. To win, we must adopt the winning attitude used in sports—teamwork, hard work, pride, determination, and competitive spirit, respect, understanding, camaraderie, and friendship. Each one of these attributes represents the commitment we all must bring to the game and to life.

The former governor and senator from the great state of Virginia is a man I have known since he was a teenager in high school. You see, I played for his father. His father made pretty good football players out of me and my teammates, because he taught us to respect each other and focus on our common goal: winning. "The Fearsome Foursome" of the Los Angeles Rams, of which I was a part, was the most dominating defensive line in all football, not because we were four individually great players, but because we were a team with one objective: to win the championship, to be the best that we could be, and together, make our mark. Teamwork is what brings success in every endeavor of life, from sports to politics.

Teams win championships. Individuals do not. America is a melting pot of cultures, religions, colors, and any number of different ideas. So is a football team. But just as that team comes together for a common goal, America has been successful because we've always come together on common principles and ultimately done what is right to guarantee life, liberty, and the pursuit of happiness for all Americans.

When I sit in front of my television these days and watch what is going on in the political arena, I am appalled at what I hear and see. What happened to respect in this country? What happened to being a good American and working with one another to solve the many problems this country faces? Why do politicians, elected to "serve" the people, seem to act on personal agendas? Every American needs to look inside himself and ask, "Am I a good American? Am I part of the team? Am I helping or hurting this country's progress? What can I do to make things better?"

While writing this foreword I received the sad news of the passing of my friend and teammate, Merlin Olsen. We played for Senator Allen's father in the 1960s and 1970s. Merlin and I came from different heritages and upbringings, but throughout our lives we had a mutual respect and a commitment to one another. For the ten years we played together side by side, we were able to dominate our game because of that respect and commitment, and because of Merlin's unwavering desire to work together to win.

I can only hope that Americans can find it in their hearts to find that same unwavering desire to help our country meet its challenges, to listen to one another, to respect each other, and to remember that we are all in this together—teammates in America, all believing in the Red, White, and Blue.

Senator Allen is exactly right: sports and Washington should go together like ham and cheese and red beans and rice. It's time for all Americans to show the determination, teamwork, and competitive spirit our country needs for an American comeback and ultimate success. This book shows how it can be done.

—David "Deacon" Jones

TIME FOR AN AMERICAN COMEBACK

When you pick up a newspaper, you'll typically find the political news on the front page and the sports section somewhere deep inside—usually just before, or just after, the lifestyle and entertainment news.

But when I consider many of our nation's problems—and the inability of our current government leaders to address them properly—I often think that many people in Washington would benefit from reading the news backwards, from reading the sports pages first.

"The sports section is the only part of the newspaper where you get the truth," my good friend Johnny Mazza likes to say. After all, it's hard to distort or manipulate the scores and the statistics. And while he says this somewhat in jest, I actually think many in Washington today could learn a lot about governing from looking at how the world of sports handles certain issues.

THE NEED FOR AN AMERICAN COMEBACK

While we all have confidence in the ability of America and Americans to succeed, I've heard from many people who are dismayed at how Washington is creating a nightmare scenario of unprecedented deficits, potentially sharp tax increases, and the likelihood of rampant inflation, all of which could destroy our children's chances of living the American Dream. America needs jobs, and you don't create real private sector jobs by coming up with more costly, massive government programs. Rather than "stimulus" spending—pork-barrel spending on steroids—we'd be better off slashing taxes and red tape to help businesses create jobs. Rather than job-killing cap-and-trade energy taxes, we need affordable American energy. Rather than government-controlled and costly health care, we want more affordable insurance premiums and decisions about our health to be between us and our doctors, not between us, our doctors, and meddling government bureaucrats.

So what does the world of sports have to say about all this? Sports teaches us that competition is a virtue, that the referees (the rule-enforcing bureaucrats) shouldn't be the focus of the game (we the players are), and that when it comes to winning and losing, as my dad coach Allen used to say, "The future is now."

Those of us here and now have the ball. We have the responsibility to improve the opportunities for success for our children and grandchildren on Team America. There is a plaque with a great quote that President Reagan gave to my father, who kept it on his desk. Since my father passed away, I've kept this plaque on my own desk. It reads:

> If not us, who?
> If not now, when?

THE GAME PLAN

So what do we need to do? Well, here are some basic principles on which everyone on Team America should be able to agree.

We need a level playing field. The referees (the Washington bureaucrats) shouldn't be lowering one basketball hoop against another, or moving the goal posts to try to ensure a government-favored outcome. It's competition that makes champions and that drives individuals and teams to excel. It's competition that creates American jobs and a dynamic economy; just as it's competition that can bring us better schools and higher standards living.

While we prize equality at the starting line, just as we prize the Declaration of Independence which affirms that "all men are created equal," we can all agree, with Navy football coach Eddie Erdelatz, that "A tie is like kissing your sister." We're all entitled to our pursuit of happiness, but we want equality of opportunity, not equality of result.

Like a coach reviewing game film, we can likely all agree that what gets measured gets better. We should never allow Washington to take our money to spend as it sees fit without the same sort of cost/benefit analysis that any business would do, or any coach would do analyzing his players and their performance.

We can know that if you want to survive as a team, you need to have a good defense. We saw that in the NCAA basketball "March

Madness" of 2010 which culminated in the matchup of defensive standouts Butler and Duke. But it's even more important when we are considering the importance of national security.

We can agree that it makes no sense to punt on first down—though Washington does that routinely when it comes to tough decisions. And we can agree that armchair quarterbacks might think they know it all—just as they think they know it all in Washington—but they never score the real touchdowns. That's done by the folks on the field, by you and me in our own real world decisions.

And there's a lot more we can learn from sports. That's why I wrote this book; and I hope we teach Washington fast, because the future is now for Team America.

CHAPTER ONE

ARMCHAIR QUARTERBACKS NEVER SCORE TOUCHDOWNS

IN WASHINGTON REDSKINS LORE, IT'S KNOWN AS "NIXON'S Play."

But it sure isn't fondly remembered the way San Francisco 49ers fans remember "The Catch" or Denver Broncos fans remember "The Drive."

Instead, "Nixon's Play" is remembered the way Cleveland Browns fans remember "The Fumble." Because "Nixon's Play" was a game-changer...in all the wrong ways.

The play was called at a crucial moment in an historic playoff game between the Washington Redskins and the San Francisco 49ers on the day after Christmas in 1971. My father, the late George

Allen, had led the Redskins to their first playoff berth in more than a quarter century in his first year as Washington's head coach.

The whole Washington area was astir. The city hadn't had a winner in any professional sport in decades, and even though the Redskins entered that playoff game as a decided underdog, expectations ran high throughout enthused Redskins fandom.

The team shared this sense of excitement. When the Redskins held a team meeting in their San Francisco hotel on the day before the game, Washington defensive tackle (and hulking, merry prankster) Manny Sistrunk came dressed as Santa Claus, much to the delight of his Redskin teammates.

Playing at a rainy Candlestick Park, Washington jumped out to an early 10–3 lead. Late in the second quarter, the Redskins drove the ball down to the 49ers' 8-yard line and looked to be on the verge of taking a 2-touchdown lead into the locker room at halftime.

At that crucial moment, Billy Kilmer called a play in the huddle that he had never before called and would never call again. It was a flanker reverse to the great Roy "Sweet Pea" Jefferson—the kind of trick play that my father usually discouraged. But it was a play that President Richard Nixon had urged the Redskins to run after seeing it work perfectly at a Washington practice earlier in the season.

The trick play fooled no one on the 49er defense that day. In fact, the play resulted in a drive-killing, 13-yard loss. Washington's subsequent field goal attempt was blocked, causing a complete shift in the game's momentum. Later, an errant snap to the Redskins' punter Mike Bragg was recovered by the 49ers for a touchdown, adding to Washington's woes. The Redskins went on to lose to the 49ers, 24–20.

After the game, my father accepted responsibility for the team's defeat. But given the game-changing significance of "Nixon's play," many people, especially in the media, blamed the president.

In a post-game locker room interview, one Redskins player expressed regret that the team had received "executive orders" to run the play. And several days after the game, Washington newspaper columnist Art Buchwald noted, "If George Allen doesn't accept any more plays from Richard Nixon, he may go down in history as one of pro football's greatest coaches."

THE FIGHTING POETS SOCIETY

As far as I know, my father didn't get any more plays from President Nixon; and he did go down in history as one of the NFL's winningest coaches. He was inducted into the Pro Football Hall of Fame in 2002. But to this day, football fans and political junkies are fascinated by "Nixon's play," the way it brought together politics and sports and highlighted an unconventional friendship.

Most people assume that my father's friendship with Richard Nixon began when he became the head coach of the Washington Redskins during President Nixon's first term. However, the two men actually met for the first time in the early 1950s at a banquet in New York City at which then Senator Nixon was the featured speaker. My father had just completed his first season as the head coach of the Whittier College Poets (yes, you read that right: the Fighting Poets must rank as the least-threatening team name of all time) after moving to Whittier from Morningside College in Sioux City, Iowa (where my parents had married). Since Nixon was a proud graduate of Whittier College and a keen sports fan, he sought out my father to congratulate him for leading the "Fighting Poets" to a 9 and 1 record.

After that meeting, Nixon was a George Allen fan and closely followed my father's coaching career. During the late 1960s, he attended games at the venerable Los Angeles Memorial Coliseum when my father was the head coach of the L.A. Rams. One of my favorite "political-football" stories from this era (other than Governor Ronald Reagan coming to a Rams practice) took place during the tumultuous 1968 election year when Nixon took a break from his presidential campaign to attend a pre-season game between the Rams and the Kansas City Chiefs. When my father learned that Nixon and his Secret Service entourage were at the game, he sent my kid brother, Bruce, who was a Rams' water boy at the time, up into the stands to give Nixon a cold drink and a Rams roster card.

Nixon invited my brother to sit with him. Everything went fine until Kansas City's quarterback Len Dawson stepped back to receive a long snap. Bruce leaped from his seat and shouted, "SHOTGUN! SHOTGUN!" The Secret Service men sprang into action. Nixon had to calm them down, saying, "Easy. This boy is talking football," and not warning about an assassination attempt.

After my father took over as Washington's head coach in 1971, Nixon rooted for the Redskins, and frequently telephoned my dad after games to offer his congratulations or condolences. After one especially difficult loss, Nixon sent an aide to our home in Great Falls, Virginia, to hand-deliver a note of encouragement. My father framed it and hung in his office at Redskins Park. The handwritten note read:

Dear George,

I saw the game on TV yesterday. A truly great team must prove that it can be great in defeat, as well as in victory. The Redskins proved they were a great team yesterday.

RMN

On a number of occasions, President Nixon invited my father to White House dinners. My father usually declined these invitations because he did not want to be distracted from his preparations for the next game. In fact, so dedicated was my father to his weekly practice regimen that he once even turned down the President's offer to hold a dinner in his honor. He said, "No, thank you," to lighting the White House Christmas tree as well.

My father did go the White House a few times; and I remember one visit in particular when our whole family attended. We were with the president in the Oval Office, having photos taken and engaging in light conversation. President Nixon reached into a desk drawer and pulled out an autographed L.A. Rams football that my father had given him years before. The two men reminisced as they looked over the ball that had been signed by Deacon Jones, Jack Snow, Roman Gabriel, Merlin Olson, Eddie Meador, Irv Cross, and other famous Rams. Nixon pointed to the signature of a little-known special teams player, Tony Guillory. The President recalled that Guillory had worn number 88, attended Lamar Tech, and blocked a Donny Anderson punt in the last minute of a dramatic comeback victory in 1967 over Vince Lombardi's Green Bay Packers.

Richard Nixon was such a loyal Redskins fan that he "pulled rank" one day during that 1971 season after Washington had lost two games in a row. He paid the team a surprise visit during a weekday practice session at Redskins Park near Dulles Airport in Virginia. In one of the most remarkable speeches ever given to any team by any president, Nixon spoke at length to the players, showing off his knowledge of the game and their abilities, and drawing parallels between their struggles and those of great military units in America's past. Nixon said:

I will go out on a limb and predict, and I have been pretty good in the field of sports, this team is going to get to the playoffs.... The reason you are going to do it is because, first, you are experienced and you are real pros, you are real great. Second, you have got the physical ability. There is no question about that. I have watched enough football to know. But third, and more important, you have got that ingredient of spirit. You really care. You want to win, and you are willing to give everything you can to see that you come back from a few, two or three, bad weeks.

After the President finished his pep talk and the team returned to its practice, my father invited Nixon to call a play during the team's intra-squad scrimmage. Nixon called the flanker reverse to Roy Jefferson—a play that some say "Tricky Dickie" drew up himself—and the play worked perfectly that day in practice.

Buoyed by the President's visit that day, the Redskins went on to win their next game, getting them back on track for their first postseason appearance since the Sammy Baugh days of the 1940s, and making President Nixon a "good luck charm" in the eyes of my father.

CALLING SHULA, SNUBBING JOEPA

Knowing the long history of their football friendship helps me better understand why my father allowed "Nixon's play" to be run in that playoff game against San Francisco. But it in no way helps me understand what Richard Nixon did next.

You see, in the aftermath of that botched play in San Francisco—in the aftermath of being blamed by some for the Redskins' reversal of fortune in that playoff game—one might think that the president of the United States would step back from calling football plays.

Yet, just over a week later, when the Miami Dolphins were preparing to play the Dallas Cowboys in Super Bowl VI, President Nixon telephoned Dolphins Coach Don Shula—*at 1:30 in the morning!*—to suggest that Miami run a particular pass play that Nixon thought Dallas would have trouble defending.

When the telephone rang at Shula's home, the legendary coach reportedly mused, "Must be some nut calling at this hour." Needless to say, Shula was quite surprised when it turned out to be the president of the United States on the other end of the phone.

After Nixon's phone call to Coach Shula came to public attention, Dallas head coach Tom Landry, a lifelong Republican, seemed miffed that his party's leader was plotting the Dallas Cowboys' demise in the Super Bowl. But Landry soon received a telegram from former president Lyndon B. Johnson, a Democrat and fellow Texan. LBJ's telegram read, "My prayers and my presence will be with you in New Orleans, although I don't plan to send in any plays."

(For the record, Miami ended up trying the play that Nixon had "phoned in" near the end of the first quarter of Super Bowl VI, but the pass to Dolphin wide receiver Paul Warfield was broken up by Dallas defensive back Mel Renfro and fell incomplete.)

While Nixon's efforts to help Miami beat the Cowboys failed—Dallas won easily, 24–3—some Texans were able to overlook the President's indiscretions because they still remembered the audacious presidential favor Nixon had bestowed upon the University of Texas Longhorns football team two years earlier.

On December 6, 1969, the Daryl Royal-coached Texas Longhorns and the Frank Broyles-coached Arkansas Razorbacks squared off in a gridiron battle that *ABC Sports* dubbed, "The Game of the Century," because it matched two unbeaten teams, led by legendary coaches, in the final regular season game of college football's centennial year. Half of the television sets in America tuned in to ABC's coverage of the game, which President Nixon attended with then Congressman George H. W. Bush of Texas. After Texas mounted a late rally to win, 15–14, President Nixon went to the Longhorns' locker room and presented the team with a presidential plaque—not authorized by the NCAA or anyone else—proclaiming them "National Champions." Nixon's audacious plaque annoyed Penn State head coach Joe Paterno, whose team had just gone undefeated for the second consecutive year.

After hearing numerous complaints from Nittany Lions fans, Nixon said he'd like to invite the Penn State team to the White House and give them a trophy for having college football's longest active winning streak. Paterno wasn't appeased. "Tell the president to take that trophy and shove it," he said. Several years later, in a commencement speech, Paterno asked, "How could Nixon know so much about college football in 1969 and so little about *Watergate* in 1973?"

A CAUTIONARY TALE

These stories about President Nixon highlight something very important about the culture of Washington—it's full of armchair quarterbacks who often get things wrong; they think they know more than they actually do, and they often imagine that they know better than anyone else.

Just as Nixon imagined that two future Hall of Fame coaches desperately needed his middle-of-the-night brainstorms in order to succeed on the NFL playing field, many people in the federal government today imagine that the American people desperately need Washington's "enlightened" intervention in their lives.

Many armchair quarterbacks in Washington today think they know more about how to raise children than moms and dads, more about how to educate students than teachers and principals, and more about how to solve community problems than the people who actually live in those communities.

Many government meddlers today think that without the "help" of Washington, Americans won't know that it's a good idea to wear a seat-belt in the car or a protective helmet on a motorcycle. They think that without the "help" of officious government nannies, Americans won't know to eat a balanced diet or to drive fuel-efficient cars.

Many know-it-alls in Washington think that they should determine the political content on radio and TV talk shows in the name of "fairness." To the disgust and opposition of many of us, they think they should decide maximum speed limits across the country and drinking ages for every state. They've even resorted to blackmailing states that are inclined to resist their all-knowing pronouncements. These federales have actually enacted a law designating which four states are allowed to have sports wagering.

More than anything else, though, many people in Washington think they know how to spend our money better than we do—so they're constantly looking for new "ways and means" to tax or direct or regulate us a little more.

The lords in Washington, in short, have a hubris problem. And the vast size, scope, and reach of the restrictions proposed by the federal government are a reflection of it. They attempt to meddle, intrude, mandate, and dictate in all aspects of our lives from the energy we use to the health care we want for our families to the money we earn.

Indeed, one of the great ironies of our time is that whenever advocates of Big Government overreach, whenever they fail to get something right, instead of stepping back and having the federal government return to those limited duties that are specifically outlined in the Constitution, advocates of Big Government typically plow ahead in Nixon-play-calling-like fashion, launching new federal initiatives designed to solve the very problems they created in the first place.

Take, for example, the great financial market collapse of 2008. Here's the way that "botched play" unfolded. First, the federal government created government-sponsored entities (Fannie Mae and Freddie Mac) managed by well-connected Washington political insiders. Then, the federal government told these agencies to start backing risky mortgages for people who did not have sufficient income to pay a mortgage on a home. When these borrowers couldn't pay their mortgages, the foreclosure crisis arose, causing housing values to collapse, and taxpayers to be stuck with trillions in new federal debt to "rescue" the financial markets.

Two things are worth noting about this financial crisis. First, it occurred because of federal manipulation of the housing market, heedless of common-sense principles of responsibility for lenders and borrowers.

Second, even though excessive government intervention into the marketplace contributed to this financial crisis in the first place, the "urgent solution" to this crisis proved to be...further government intervention into the marketplace.

Thus, to this day, no one from Washington or Wall Street has convinced the owners of small businesses why their tax dollars should have been used to bail out the poor business decisions by big financial moguls. It is no wonder people have so little confidence in the federal government. It spent billions bailing out automobile manufacturers, banks, brokers, and credit card companies—while responsible taxpaying families, homeowners, and small business owners got stuck paying these bills.

MR. JEFFERSON'S QUARTERBACK

Lest anyone get the wrong impression, I want to make it clear that I believe the federal government has an important role to play in American life. And I recognize that our nation's capital has many knowledgeable, experienced, and articulate people who are sincerely striving to advance noble ideals and offer practical solutions for our country.

Moreover, I take pride in my accomplishments in government, working to improve the opportunities, security, and prosperity for the people I served as Governor, as Senator, as Congressman, and as Delegate in the Virginia General Assembly. So I in no way want to imply that public service is an inherently disreputable or "shady" line of work.

I do, however, agree with Thomas Jefferson (whose seat I once held in the Virginia House of Delegates) that "the government that governs least governs best," and that the closer a level of government is to the people, the more reflective and responsive it is to the will of the governed.

My favorite description of the role of government was expressed by President Jefferson in his First Inaugural Address in 1801. He defined "the sum of good government" as:

> Still one thing more, fellow citizens—a wise and frugal Government, which shall restrain men from injuring one another, shall leave them otherwise free to regulate their own pursuits of industry and improvement, and shall not take from the mouth of labor the bread it has earned.

The reason to adhere to this philosophy, the reason I have so much appreciation for "a wise and frugal government" that exists primarily to "restrain men from injuring one another," isn't simply because I studied history and law at "Mr. Jefferson's University." It's also partly because I played on the University of Virginia football team as an undergrad and on the UVA rugby club team as a law student.

I realize that that last statement may seem odd—and I say it half in jest. But I've spent the better part of my life with one foot in the world of sports and the other foot in the world of politics, and among the things that I've discovered is this: *Washington could stand to learn a great deal from the characteristics of the world of sports.*

That's right, Washington could stand to learn a whole lot from the lessons taught in sports, from the enduring principles found in sports. Because many of the most difficult and most pressing problems that confound even the smartest minds in Washington are the kinds of problems that the sports world typically manages to address much more easily and effectively.

Take, for example, the issue of race. In the wake of Barack Obama's phenomenal election in 2008, Americans of all political persuasions have rightly celebrated the historic ascendancy of an African-American to the presidency. I worked for John McCain in the campaign, and was still personally moved watching Barack Obama and his family on the night of the election as he gave his victory speech at Chicago's Grant Park. All of us who saw that victory speech were watching the inspirational fulfillment and embodiment of the American Dream in the world of politics. The election of an African-American president truly was—and is—an important milestone in our nation's political history, and we are right to trumpet its significance in the course of human events.

African-Americans ascended to the top of the sports world long before they ascended to the top of the political world. In the 1930s, Jesse Owens became arguably the greatest Olympic sprinter of all time at the Berlin Games (much to Adolf Hitler's aggravation). In the 1940s, Joe Louis held the world heavyweight boxing crown longer than any boxer before or since. In the 1950s, Jim Brown established himself as arguably the greatest football running back of all time, first for Syracuse University and then for the NFL's Cleveland Browns. In the 1960s, Bill Russell led the Boston Celtics to the longest-running period of dominance in professional basketball, playing against the likes of Elgin Baylor, Oscar Robertson, Wilt Chamberlin, and other African-American NBA stars. In the 1970s, Atlanta Braves slugger Hank Aaron became the all-time home run king in Major League Baseball. In the 1980s, Michael Jordan began what would become the greatest professional basketball career in history. In the 1990s, Tiger Woods did the same in golf (following in the wake of other "minorities" such as Lee Elder, Lee Trevino, and Chi Chi Rodriguez). And here in the twenty-first century, Venus and Serena Williams have excelled at the game that Richmond's Arthur Ashe loved, becoming the greatest "sister act" of all time in professional women's tennis.

The reason I recount this long (yet greatly abbreviated) list of athletic achievement by African-Americans is not, in any way, to diminish Barack Obama's electoral achievement. It is, instead, to make the point that black athletic achievement played a major role in helping change American attitudes about race. Black athletic achievement helped set in motion many of the positive changes that have taken place in American life. The characteristics of sports paved the way for many of the political milestones we celebrate today.

Indeed, interestingly, the desegregation of American schools occurred *after* the successful integration of the races in Major League Baseball and other professional sports. The passage of the Voting Rights Act occurred *after* black athletes had been voted recipients of various All-Star and Most Valuable Player and Rookie of the Year awards. And the adoption of the Civil Rights Act occurred *after* numerous black athletes like Jackie Robinson had the opportunity to excel on the playing field with white athletes.

To be sure, sports weren't the only cultural influence positively affecting race relations. And the path to racial equality in sports was, at times, anything but smooth. For example, many southern colleges were slow to give black players a chance to play on their teams well after the professional sports leagues had been racially integrated. But all of this began to change in college basketball when a Texas Western team with an all-black starting line-up beat Adolph Rupp's all-white Kentucky Wildcats team in the 1966 NCAA championship. And all of this began to change in college football after Bear Bryant's all-white Alabama team got trounced in its 1970 home opener by an integrated University of Southern California team led by Trojans' running back, Sam "the Bam" Cunningham. Reflecting on the impact of Cunningham's legendary performance in that game, Crimson Tide assistant coach Jerry Claiborne observed, "Sam Cunningham did more to integrate Alabama in 60 minutes that night than Martin Luther King had accomplished in 20 years."

While Claiborne's words were grossly unfair towards Dr. King, his legitimate point should not be missed. Time and time again, the world of sports has been a leader in helping our nation confront, and overcome, racial bias. Time and time again, the world of sports has greatly helped our nation see the horrible unfairness of racial discrimination. And the sports world has been able to play this leadership role for one vitally instructive reason: *The world of sports is a meritocracy.*

The world of sports rewards excellence. It honors genuine achievement. It celebrates greatness. Sports teams do not care about a player's religion, race, ethnicity, or place of origin. All a team cares about is whether a player can punt, pass, kick, run, tackle, hit, catch, pitch, dribble, shoot, jump, rebound, skate, evade, elude, block, or defend well enough to help the team win.

Mitch Albom, the best-selling author who has written about sports for many years, understands this well. In one of his columns written after the 2008 election, Albom compared his no-big-deal reaction to the election of a black man as president to the no-big-deal reaction that 1960s running back Gale Sayers (whom my father drafted in 1965) gave to the coaching staff of the Chicago Bears when Sayers learned he would be rooming with a white player, Brian Piccolo (as depicted in the movie, *Brian's Song*). Albom wrote:

> Being a sportswriter may not get you much—besides a decent seat and mustard on your tie—but it does prepare you for race relations.... [A]s a white sportswriter...you get accustomed to talking to black Americans doing better than you financially, being better known, more widely respected. You get accustomed to black coaches making trades, black executives returning your phone calls—or not.
>
> The music you hear is often not your music. The slang in the locker room is often not your slang. In the case of Latino or Japanese players, it may not even be your language. But you know what? You do your job. Everyone else does his or her job. And pretty soon all that stuff fades to the background....
>
> Maybe, in writing about a world where black people and white people dress together, shower together, block and tackle for each other and douse each other with champagne, we sportswriters have been exposed to something progressive. If so, I can tell those who are nervous [about the election of our first black president] that there is nothing to

worry about. That world works the way you want a world to work. Get the job done, and everyone respects you.

My experiences growing up in a football family were very similar to those Albom described. In the sports world that I knew growing up, race did not matter. Going all the way back to his first team—the 1948 Morningside College team—my father always coached both black and white players, and he typically had star players of both races. On the Chicago Bears teams my dad coached, Dick Butkus and Gale Sayers were cheered. On the L.A. Rams teams he led, Roman Gabriel and Deacon Jones were the greats. On my dad's Redskins teams, Charlie Taylor, Dave Butz, Diron Talbert, Ken Houston, Brig Owens, and Billy Kilmer all carried on like one, big, happy family—especially during summer training camp (which, incidentally, was held in Carlisle, Pennsylvania, on the home field of Jim Thorpe, the great American Indian pro football star who also won the Olympic decathlon).

Race, ethnicity, origins, and religious persuasion did not matter. What mattered was one's ability to help the team win. In fact, so "unconscious" of race was my upbringing in a football family that, in a strange sort of way, I entered adulthood—and probably even public life—not fully comprehending the full gravity of our nation's struggle for racial equality. Since I had so rarely witnessed extreme racial discrimination growing up around professional football, I did not grasp, until much later, the full magnitude of racial strife occurring in other parts of America during my childhood years.

Indeed, I remember attending a Civil Rights Pilgrimage through Alabama in 2003, while I was serving in the U.S. Senate. Over the course of several days, the folks taking part in this pilgrimage visited many of the famous pivotal historic sites in Birmingham, Montgomery, and Selma. We heard presentations from civil rights leaders like Congressman John Lewis, who had experienced many of these violent events firsthand. And we watched old film clips and television footage showing street conflicts and the heartless mistreatment and repression of people due to their skin color.

As I took part in this pilgrimage, I was both moved and shocked: moved by the extraordinary courage of those who peaceably resisted racial discrimination, yet shocked by just how alien my childhood experiences growing up around pro football in Chicago and Los Angeles were to those of white and black kids growing up amid serious racial strife in the Deep South during those same years.

Like Albom, I had found that the world of sports, whatever its imperfections, works by some simple rules: Get the job done, and everyone respects you. Prove that you have what it takes to succeed, and no one cares whether you're black, brown, or white, whether you're native or immigrant, whether you're blue-blood or working class. That's the essence of a merit-based system. And that's the American way, at least as the world of sports sees it. More importantly, though, it is a meritocracy which we should aspire to imitate in our society.

Of course, the world of sports isn't just a meritocracy—it's a highly objective meritocracy. The world of sports likes keeping score. It appreciates statistical comparisons. It relishes clear-cut outcomes. The sports world is not troubled by having winners and losers—so long as everyone plays by the rules. In fact, the world of sports recognizes that failure can sometimes build character, that failure can often be a precursor to extraordinary success. In sports, no one would tolerate "redistributing" victories, points, or yardage to less successful teams or players.

Sadly, the world of Washington seems to have a completely different playbook. While our founding documents uphold ideals like "all men are created equal," far too often people in Washington today act as though certain people are "more equal" than others.

The culture of Washington today is elitist. It favors the insider. It caters to the rich and powerful and well-connected.

Far too often, the culture of Washington accepts mediocrity. It resists accountability. It discourages personal responsibility and encourages dependency on government. It tolerates or makes excuses for unproductive, or even counter-productive, behavior.

The culture of Washington foments grievances and division. It fosters suspicions of others. It believes Uncle Sam should play favorites and pick winners, that Washington should take from those it lightly regards and "give" to those it highly regards.

The culture of Washington, in short, is very often at odds with the culture of sports—and our nation is the worse for it.

A "SPORTSMAN'S SENSIBILITY"

Over the course of this book, we will explore these contrasting characteristics and the clash of these cultures. And we'll be exploring how sports teach lessons that can help federal and state government policymakers improve job opportunities, reform education, improve our energy freedom, strengthen national security, and rein in activist judges, government spending, and debt.

It may seem strange to assert that many problems in the mostly serious arena of government could be addressed effectively by drawing upon instructive solutions found in the often playful arena of sports.

But I know from firsthand experience that a background in sports can be extremely useful in governing; many of the most impressive men I have met in government have been athletes. For example, Cabinet Secretary Jack Kemp was an All-Star, record-setting quarterback for the Buffalo Bills. Congressman Steve Largent is a Hall of Fame wide receiver who starred for the Seattle Seahawks. Senator Jim Bunning is a Hall of Fame baseball pitcher who played for the Philadelphia Phillies and Detroit Tigers. Congressman Jim Ryan was an Olympic medalist in track who once held the world record in the mile run. Senator Bill Bradley is a Hall of Fame basketball player who starred for the New York Knicks. And Congressman J. C. Watts was a star quarterback for the University of Oklahoma football team (and my daughter Tyler's favorite speaker).

Part of what made these ex-jocks good public servants is that they brought to their work a "sportsman's sensibility." That is, they had an almost instinctive sense that the principles and attributes that promote fair play in sports would be the same principles and attributes that ensure fairness in government.

Moreover, athletes know that one must master the fundamentals in order to succeed in sports, these athletes-turned-legislators understood the need to be "fundamentally sound" when it came to governing. They were well versed in the "founding principles" upon which our nation was built—ideas of separation of powers, checks and balances, the rule of law, the consent of the governed, and equal justice under the law—and they sought to uphold these principles at every turn.

Clearly, I had the honor of serving with many "fundamentally sound" policymakers who had no background in sports—and I acknowledge that just because someone has a "sportsman's sensibility" doesn't necessarily mean he or she is cut out for public office.

I remember, for example, a rather amusing story from when I was Chairman of the Senate Republican Campaign Committee during the 2004 election cycle. A big part of my job was to recruit, assist, and counsel good candidates to run for Senate seats being contested that year in various states. This task was easier in traditionally Republican states like South Carolina than in traditionally Democratic states like Illinois. Republican U.S.

Senator Peter Fitzgerald decided not to run for reelection, desiring to lead a more normal life with his family. Our brightest, best recruit was former Illinois Governor Jim Edgar. He had a proven, honest record and was highly respected throughout Illinois. He certainly would have won if he had decided to "go for it." But Governor Edgar decided against uprooting and disrupting his life. Then, due to a media frenzy, the eventual Republican nominee had to drop out of the open seat contest. Still, I thought we might have us a "ringer" for the U.S. Senate race in Illinois when Mike Ditka, the beloved Chicago Bears legend, showed an interest in running against the Democrats' nominee—an up-and-coming state senator named Barack Obama.

When I went to meet Coach Ditka at his restaurant in Chicago, the news media had somehow caught wind of my visit. There were reporters and camera crews literally hiding behind the restaurant's dumpsters, waiting to ambush me with questions when I got out of my car. I managed to evade the media to get inside to talk to Coach Ditka; and he and his wife took me to an upstairs room where we could talk freely and confidentially, without disruption.

Coach Ditka and my family go way back. My father signed him to play for the Bears when I was a kid. My mother greatly admired his toughness and would often say to me growing up, "Drink your milk like Mike Ditka so that you can have strong bones." As a youngster, I learned some interesting words and phrases from Ditka that I had never heard before (and can't repeat in polite company). So, seeing Coach Ditka at his restaurant that day brought back many great memories as well as a lot of respect and admiration.

Since Coach Ditka is a family friend, I felt a special obligation to be sure that he knew all the rules of the political game. I was convinced that Coach Ditka could bring a tough, passionate, and refreshing candor to the U.S. Senate, but I also wanted to be sure that he knew what running for the Senate entailed, what being a senator was like, and what it would take to get elected. Coach Ditka asked a playbook of good questions—and made several hilarious wisecracks. At one point, he joked that if he were elected senator, one of his first actions on the Senate floor would be to stroll across the aisle and "deck" a particular senator he disliked.

Unfortunately, Coach Ditka had some tall challenges to over-come in waging a Senate race. He had moved his permanent resi-dency from Illinois. He had recently entered into some business dealings (promoting a new line of clothing) that he'd have to sus-pend. He would not be able to appear in television commercials for business (I explained how even Pete Coors could not be in Coors ads in Colorado during his Senate race). And Iron Mike Ditka and (especially) his wife had some very serious concerns about the per-ils of running for office and the invasion of their privacy.

His wife sat and listened intently to our conversation in the restaurant that evening. After smoking through a pack of Marlboro Lights, she finally interjected, "Look at him." Pointing to me in my dark suit and tie, she said, "Mike, if you were in the Senate, you'd have to dress like that every day."

Coach Ditka turned and asked me, "Is that really true?"

I looked over at Coach Ditka, who was dressed in an open-collared, Hawaiian-style shirt, and replied, "Well…yes…you probably would have to wear a suit and tie on most official busi-ness as a U.S. Senator. Senator Ben 'Nighthorse' Campbell gets away with wearing a bolo tie because of his American Indian her-itage, but on the Senate floor, one has to wear a coat and tie." It was evident to me that this news didn't sit too well with Coach Ditka. "Think of it this way, Coach," I appealed to him, "dressing up for the Senate would be like wearing a coat and tie on road trips with the Bears." The coach seemed to appreciate that analogy.

But it didn't help. Ditka's wife turned to her husband, and said, "See, Mike, you don't want do this." And she was right. The standard everyday "uniform" of the U.S. Senate just added to the pile of reasons Coach Ditka had *not* to run for the U.S Senate in 2004. Besides, he wanted to honor his contractual obligations and maintain the privacy of his family's life. The hopes of Illinois Republicans to get the Bears legend to run for public office were sunk by Ditka's honorable sense of keeping promises.

So, not every sportsman is cut out for public office. But a healthy knowledge of sports can be quite useful in public service.

The insightful sportswriter and ESPN commentator, Michael Wilbon, made this point in a column awhile back. "Going back to Dwight D. Eisenhower, who played college football at Army and was a golf fanatic, every U.S. president has been anywhere from somewhat involved to immersed in sports at some point in his life," Wilbon wrote. He then recounted that John F. Kennedy loved playing touch football at family gatherings, Bush "41" played baseball at Yale, Bush "43" once owned the Texas Rangers baseball team, and Gerald R. Ford starred on the University of Michigan football team.

Interestingly, Wilbon's tone shifted when he referenced Jimmy Carter. Recalling the controversial U.S. boycott of the 1980 Olympics, Wilbon wrote, "Carter didn't have enough appreciation for the Olympics, and you see how that worked out for him."

HAIL TO THE REDSKINS, HAIL TO THE CHIEF

While having a "sportsman's sensibility" doesn't guarantee success in politics, it does provide some unexpected advantages to those who serve in public office or who are interested or involved in politics. What sorts of lessons does Washington need to learn from the world of sports?

There are all sorts of elaborate ways to describe these ideas, but in the course of writing this book, I've often asked myself how my dad would communicate these lessons were he still with us. Here's the way the great Deacon Jones described my father's methods in a speech he gave at the Pro Football Hall of Fame:

> My experience with George Allen began in 1966 when he was hired to lead the Los Angeles Rams out of the depths of despair. I remember walking into the locker room that first morning and seeing little signs plastered all over the place. Little sayings that you might find pasted on a grammar school wall. One-liners that seemed ridiculous. The Rams had not had a winning season since 1958, and we needed a miracle worker not a schoolteacher. We all looked at each other and shrugged. But, then we met Coach Allen. And that was exactly what we got—a miracle worker of the utmost degree.
>
> He drove us to make the most of ourselves and he made us winners. Finishing the season with an 8 and 6 record. And we learned to love those little sayings of George Allen.

This is not to insinuate that the business of governing can be reduced to a handful of pithy sayings. But in describing what I think Washington most needs to learn from the world of sports, I plan to draw upon some of the favorite sayings of Coach George Allen and President Ronald Reagan and a number of other great leaders, including some of our founding fathers. I think you will find that many of these sayings capture a big idea rather well. And I think you will find that many of these little sayings will allow us to reverse the flow of "Nixon's play"—in other words, politics needs to learn a whole lot more from the world of sports, while politicians don't have much to teach the sporting world.

Get ready, my friends. Put on your game face. Buckle your chin-straps. Because the next chapter will examine one of the most important lessons of all. And it will begin, appropriately enough, with the most noble (and most difficult) loss on the football field that a future U.S. Congressman from Nebraska ever suffered.

CHAPTER TWO

A TIE IS LIKE KISSING YOUR SISTER

WHEN MIAMI'S HISTORIC ORANGE BOWL STADIUM CLOSED down for good in 2007, *NBC Sports* put together a list of the greatest college football games ever played at the storied 70-year-old facility. At the top of their list, ahead of even Doug Flutie's miraculous game-ending "Hail Mary" touchdown pass for Boston College, the folks at NBC placed the 1984 Orange Bowl game played by Nebraska and Miami. And it's hard to argue with their decision. While Flutie's famous last-second pass showed the power of prayer, the ending of the 1984 Orange Bowl game was a tribute to exemplary character.

In 1983, the Nebraska Cornhuskers had one of the highest-scoring teams in college football history. Led by head coach (and future U.S. Congressman) Tom Osborne, the Cornhuskers won most of their games by lopsided margins: 84–13 over Minnesota, 72–29 over Iowa State, 67–13 over Kansas, 63–7 over Syracuse. To give you an idea of just how prolific Nebraska's offense was, in its 69–19 win over Colorado, the Cornhuskers scored seven touchdowns in one quarter!

Nebraska finished the regular season 12–0 and ranked No. 1 in all the polls. Tailback Mike Rozier won the Heisman Trophy. Several of his teammates, including wingback Irving Fryer and quarterback Turner Gill, joined him as All-Americans.

So intimidating were the Cornhuskers that when a reporter asked "The Diesel" John Riggins about the Washington Redskins' very challenging schedule that season, the always-quotable NFL running back replied, "Hey, at least we don't have to play Nebraska."

The Cornhuskers rolled into the Orange Bowl on a 22-game winning streak. They were 11-point favorites over an upstart Miami Hurricanes team led by Howard Schnellenberger, a colorful head coach who had once assisted my father with the L.A. Rams and had also coached under the revered Bear Bryant at Alabama.

Miami hadn't played in a major bowl game in more than three decades and didn't have a single All-American on its roster. Nevertheless, the Hurricanes jumped out to an early 17–0 lead, thanks to the pinpoint passing of its freshman quarterback Bernie Kosar.

The Cornhuskers fought back and eventually tied the score with their famous "fumblerooski" touchdown play by offensive lineman Dean Steinkuhler, only to fall behind again to the relentless Hurricanes. Trailing by seven with less than a minute to play, Nebraska scored on a remarkable fourth-and-long 24-yard run for a touchdown by Jeff Smith to pull within a point, 31–30. This set up one of the most agonizing extra-point decisions any football coach has ever had to make.

THE BIG DECISION

Since the NCAA had yet to adopt overtime play in college football—that would come more than a decade later—Nebraska Coach Tom Osborne essentially had two options. He could kick for one point, have the game end in a tie, and virtually guarantee Nebraska a national championship since a 12-0-1 Cornhusker team would finish the season as the nation's only undefeated team. Or he could play to win on a two-point conversion, risking defeat, and the national championship, in the process.

Osborne chose to play for the win. But Nebraska's two-point conversion pass play fell incomplete, giving Miami a 31–30 victory and its first national championship. "I don't think you go for a tie in that case," Osborne explained afterward. "We wanted an undefeated season and a clear-cut national championship. I don't think any of our players would be satisfied backing into it with a P. A. T. [point after touchdown]."

Some observers marveled at the courage of Osborne's decision to go for two. But the "old school" Nebraska coach downplayed its significance. "It wasn't any act of heroism or great fortitude," Osborne said. "You play to win—that's how you win the national championship."

Osborne would go on to win three national championships for Nebraska, and to retire in 1997 as one of the winningest coaches in college football history. But it would be his determination to win with honor (or not at all) that would define Osborne's coaching legacy more than any single achievement.

Meanwhile, that 1984 Orange Bowl catapulted Miami into the upper stratosphere of the college football world. Over the next two decades, the Hurricanes won four more national championships. And they might have won another had the 1988 'Canes converted a last-minute, two-point play in an eerily similar situation against Notre Dame. In that midseason classic, which some called the "Catholics v. Convicts" game, Miami lost by the identical score (31–30) and went on to finish the year ranked second behind eventual national champion Notre Dame.

"TIE ONE FOR THE GIPPER"

Lest one get the wrong idea, some coaches who've gone for broke rather than settling for a tie have not only won respect, but have also won the game to boot. Conversely, some who've settled for a tie—even when doing so helped them "win" a championship—have ended up receiving ridicule rather than respect.

That, at least, is what happened to Notre Dame's head coach Ara Parseghian after his No. 1 Notre Dame team tied No. 2 Michigan State in a low-scoring defensive struggle in 1966. In that game, Notre Dame had the ball on its own 30-yard line with more than a minute to play and the score tied 10–10. The Irish needed to drive the ball 40 yards to be able to set up a game-winning field goal, but Parseghian decided to run out the clock instead because he did not want to risk a turnover that could give Michigan State a chance to score.

"We'd fought hard to come back and tie it up," Parseghian subsequently explained. "After all that, I didn't want to risk giving it to them cheap.... I wasn't going to do a jackass thing like that."

Parseghian's play-it-safe, settle-for-a-tie, end-of-game strategy left many sports fans feeling cheated. For years afterward, Notre

Dame detractors criticized Parseghian's overly cautious decision. Thus, even though Notre Dame's strategy "worked"—the Irish finished the year ranked No. 1—it still came at a cost to the team's reputation. In fact, many years later, when *Sports Illustrated* published a feature story about that memorable 1966 game, the article described this historic contest as the game when the not-so Fighting Irish chose to "Tie one for the Gipper."

BOMBS BURSTING IN AIR

The sports world despises ties. It deplores draws. It detests stalemates. Equal outcomes leave everyone unsatisfied, which is why many in the world of sports have repeated a line first uttered by Navy football coach Eddie Erdelatz after his team's 1953 game against Duke ended in a scoreless draw: *A tie is like kissing your sister.*

The world of athletic competition dislikes ties so much that virtually every sport has developed often elaborate rules for determining a winner if the game is knotted at the end of regulation. Some of these tie-breaking methods are controversial, such as penalty kicks in soccer and shootouts in hockey. And these tiebreakers occasionally lengthen games to almost absurd degrees.

For example, the New York Mets beat the Atlanta Braves 16–13 in an extra-inning night game in 1985 that went on so long the Braves had to send to the plate pitcher Rick Camp, a career .060 hitter, because they had no position players left to bat. Amazingly, Camp hit a two-out, two-strike home run—the only one he ever hit in the big leagues!—to tie the score in the bottom of the eighteenth inning and extend the game even further.

Eventually, the Mets won; but since the game had been delayed twice by rain, the extra-inning marathon didn't end until well after three o'clock in the morning. At that point, the strange night became even stranger.

The game had begun on the Fourth of July; and the Braves had promised their fans that there would be a huge fireworks display at the stadium immediately after the game's conclusion. Even though only 100 or so fans had endured all the way to the end, the Braves felt a promotional obligation to shoot off the fireworks. So, in the wee morning hours of July 5, 1985, many Atlanta residents were awakened by the sound of "bombs bursting in air"—as the Braves offered the grand finale to one of the most bizarre games in major league baseball history.

HATING TIES, BUT LOVING EQUALITY

Flawed or not, sports tie-breakers are almost always considered better than the alternative—playing games that settle nothing. Thus, the only time most sports currently allow a game to end in a tie is when player safety could be seriously jeopardized if play were to continue. This is why regular season NFL games are halted after a 15-minute overtime period if neither team scores, and why boxing matches sometimes end in a draw.

Yet, here's where it really gets interesting. *The sports world despises ties, but prizes equality of opportunity.*

In sports, equality of outcome—a tie—is something to avoid. But having a "level playing field" is an essential part of the game. Typically, Washington gets this exactly backward. When folks in Washington take about "equality" they're not usually talking about a "level playing field," they're talking about trying to rig the game for a contrived outcome or result. In their manipulative, pity-the-poor-loser, let's-give-everyone-a-participation-trophy way of thinking, many in Washington believe that our society's ultimate goal should be to have the federal government redistribute resources "from each according to his ability, to each according to his need." In their minds, this would produce a society in which no one would be rich or poor—we'd all end up more or less "equal."

Now, of course, sharing resources, being generous, and helping educational, medical, research, religious, and other charities are things families do all the time—and that's commendable. In sports it might be called "teamwork." The problem is that in Washington the high ideals of charity and generosity and teamwork become social engineering, bureaucratic dictates, and economic confiscation. The goal is to produce an equality of outcome; the actual result is to stifle and inhibit freedom, vitality, and self-reliance.

Human nature shows that people will not strive as long, work as hard, study as diligently, innovate as readily, risk as freely, care as passionately, sacrifice as willingly, or produce as much if they know that, in the end, the fruits or rewards or honors or acclaim will be re-distributed evenly to others.

In sporting contests, no boxer ever puts on his gloves imagining how great it would be to have the match end in a draw. No football player ever buckles his chinstrap before the opening kickoff hoping the game will eventually end in a tie. And no sprinter ever steps into the starting blocks dreaming of how nice it would be for every runner to cross the finish line at the exact same instant... holding hands!

No, we are all propelled—and compelled—to strive harder and work faster and do better because we want to excel. We want to achieve. We want to be the best. Like a NASCAR driver racing at Daytona, we want to start our engines and put the pedal to the metal—winding up on Victory Lane.

And we want to succeed not just for our own gain and glory, but so that we can share the fruits of our success with those we love.

Abraham Lincoln understood this principle. He once said, "Let not him who is houseless pull down the house of another; but let him labor diligently and build one for himself, thus by example assuring that his own shall be safe from violence when built."

Sadly, many folks in Washington today do not understand what Mr. Lincoln found so plainly true. They love to attack the successful, "the rich," "the top five percent of all earners" as greedy and uncaring.

To be sure, our capitalist system produces a few fraudulent self-promoters and con men. But our free market system produces far more Tom Osborne, Rich Gannon, Jerry Rice, Tim Tebow, Kurt Warner, Ronde Barber, Drew Brees, Walter Peyton, and Rod Woodson types—people of character, achievement, and distinction who would rather compete honorably, and sometimes lose, than participate in an economic system where no one ever succeeds or fails... or gets to enjoy the fruits of their hard work, diligence, and creativity.

A LEVEL PLAYING FIELD

We do have to recognize that many of the "winners" in our capitalist system come to the game with natural advantages—as some athletes have natural advantages of speed or size or coordination, or, if they come from a well-to-do background, perhaps access to elite coaching—that they use to achieve excellence. But our capitalist system also produces lots of Deacon Jones types—compelling "underdogs" who are convinced that they can succeed beyond all others' expectations if they're simply given a chance to prove what they can do.

I first met Deacon Jones at the L.A. Rams training camp soon after my father took over as head coach of the team in 1966. Deacon didn't quite know what to make of my father at first, but he and our family eventually became very close. In fact, my feisty sister Jennifer, a Features Reporter for the NFL Network, named one of her sons Deacon. All this happened because my father was the first coach who ever gave Deacon the opportunity to compete on a "level playing field." As Deacon said at my father's induction into the Pro Football Hall of Fame: "I give 100 percent of the credit for developing my career to Coach Allen. At the time, I did not like white people. I was dealing with segregation and tokenism. Then I met Coach Allen. He brought about the only level playing field I ever had, and all the things I was really upset about in my life switched just like that."

The man who became known as the "Secretary of Defense" grew up in the days of the segregated South. Black athletes of his era were not recruited by the powerhouse teams from the Southeastern Conference (SEC). Instead, he played at two historical black colleges where the football facilities were meager in comparison to those of the all-white colleges. Deacon began at South Carolina State, but had to drop out because he participated in a civil rights protest (which was not allowed), and finished his college career at the school now known as Mississippi Valley State.

When Deacon made his way to the NFL as a fourteenth round draft pick, he was eager to measure himself against the more celebrated players coming out of well known college programs. He knew he could play. And he certainly knew how to deliver an original quote. When he was asked about the head slap, his signature move for getting around an offensive lineman to sack the quarterback, he said, "The head slap was not my invention, but Rembrandt, of course, did not invent painting."

Deacon wanted an opportunity to prove that he belonged in the NFL. He wasn't looking for special favors or kid glove treatment. He wasn't afraid of head-to-head competition. All Deacon needed was a chance—an "equal" chance—to prove what he could do on the football field.

I intentionally use the term "equal" here because Deacon Jones's understanding of "equality" is right in line with all those in sports who understand the concept of a "level playing field." Equality, in this sense, is to be prized. Because the only way you can have a fair competition is if the rules are the same for everybody. The only way one can truly measure oneself against a competitor is if the baskets are the same height at both ends of the floor, the goals are the same size at both ends of the hockey rink, and the playing surface is not tilted to give one side an unfair advantage over the other.

The sports world's understanding of equality is right in line with the way our nation's founding fathers defined "equality." To their credit, the founders had a "starting line" understanding of equality rather than the "finish line" definition found in today's Official Washington Insider's Dictionary. Note, for example, that the Declaration of Independence says that all men "are *created* equal" and that we are all endowed by our Creator with certain inalienable rights, including "life, liberty, and the *pursuit* of happiness."

In saying that "all men are *created* equal," the founders were saying that all of us have equal dignity as human beings, and that all of us are entitled, therefore, to equal justice under the law. Translated into football-speak, one might say that the founders believed that the enforcement of "illegal procedure"—and the penalty for this infraction—ought to be the same no matter who commits the foul.

Similarly, when the founders said that all men have the right to "*pursue* happiness," they meant it in the same sense that the sports world holds that every team or every competitor has the right to *pursue* victory. The founders, obviously, weren't promising anyone a rose garden...or a post-championship trip to the White

House rose garden. Nor were they insinuating that everyone possesses an equal measure of the qualities needed for success (not that "experts" in Washington would be able to reliably predict those qualities). After all, from a "raw talent" standpoint, David had less strength than Goliath, the fabled Tortoise had less speed than the Hare, and the Hickory High basketball team in *Hoosiers* had far fewer elite athletes than its Indiana state championship opponent. Yet, we all love when underdogs succeed. And the fact that the "underdogs" succeeded on a level playing field only served to make their highly improbable victories all the more compelling. That's why most Americans were sentimentally cheering for the New Orleans Saints to win the Super Bowl while admiring the character of Peyton Manning.

Now, the founders weren't perfect. While they defined "equality" and many other terms superbly, they didn't always live up to their lofty ideals. Our nation had to endure four score and seven years of slavery as a result; and it took another hundred plus years of striving for a more perfect union to finally and forever end discriminatory laws and practices that had been enacted in slavery's wake.

To his great credit, Martin Luther King Jr. understood the promise of the American Dream. Rather than deriding our founding fathers, Dr. King actually rooted his appeal for justice and change in the founders' ideals, saying that it was high time for a nation of free people to fully live up to the lofty principles of those who had once proclaimed that "all men are created equal."

As Dr. King noted, "When the architects of our republic wrote the magnificent words of the Constitution and the Declaration of Independence, they were signing a promissory note to which every American was to fall heir."

For Deacon Jones and Jackie Robinson and numerous other black athletes, that "promissory note" guaranteed equal opportunity—not equal outcomes. A level playing field means everyone can claim the rewards of their hard work and success; it means that people can't legitimately claim they were wronged if they don't succeed; it encourages hard work and responsibility and the competitive spirit athletes need to overcome adversity, and it helps prevent us from becoming a nation of bellyachers, whiners, and sore losers.

Some may say, "Yes, a level playing field is great when we're talking about a game, but not when 'failure' means losing your job or your home or your business. We need a 'compassionate' government that cares for the poor and downtrodden."

You know what—that's partly right. We do need government to acknowledge and account for certain disadvantages people have—and I'll deal with that in the next chapter. But before we get there, I think we need to dwell long and hard on the importance of the level playing field, because the first and most important function of government is to provide equal justice. To that end, government needs to be an impartial referee and not favor one group or interest over another. Another word for that is fairness—and that's the American way.

Unfortunately, pressure to tilt the playing field can come from either side of the political aisle. Liberals, as we know, seem to think this is what government is all about—ensuring equality of outcome, or at least tilting the playing field to reward favored groups. But big business, and its conservative and liberal friends, often appears to believe in free competition only on its terms, lobbying government for rules and regulations that actually discourage competitors. In government, everyone will say they agree with "justice" and "fairness," but what really matters is whether they see justice and fairness as equality of opportunity, a level playing field, or as an excuse to use government power to favor some groups over others.

WHY MOST COACHES VOTE REPUBLICAN

Since the "level-playing field" principle is so ingrained in those involved in competitive sports, and so often violated by those who advocate for "liberal" intrusive, centralized government programs, a noteworthy majority of athletes and coaches who get involved in politics do so as Republicans—or at least that's what Steve Kornacky argued in a provocative 2009 column in *The Wall Street Journal* entitled, "Why Your Football Coach Votes Republican."

After citing a long list of prominent football coaches and athletes who have contributed to GOP candidates, spoken at Republican events, or run for public office in recent years, Kornacky provides insight from several of these gridiron heroes into why so many of them vote Republican. For example, in passages about Lou Holtz and J. C. Watts, Kornacky writes:

> Mr. Holtz, who coached Notre Dame to its last national championship in 1988, draws a parallel between the standards and rules that most coaches set for their players and the Republican vision of how American society ought to operate.
>
> "You aren't entitled to anything. You don't inherit anything. You get what you earn—your position on the team," Mr. Holtz said. "You're treated like everybody else. You're held accountable for your actions. You understand that your decisions affect other people on that team.... There's winners, there's losers, and there's competitiveness."...
>
> [The Honorable J. C.] Watts argues there's a link between football and Republicanism.
>
> "The values that Republicans espouse in terms of capitalism, free enterprise, responsibility, working hard,

sacrifice and commitment—that message probably resonates with the majority of athletes a lot more," said Watts,
who retired in 2003 after eight years in Congress.

To his credit, Kornacky is careful not to overstate his case. For
example, he notes:

> There's no evidence that coaches with a conservative
> bent are better coaches or more likely to get jobs. . . . And
> when Mr. Obama was running . . . several African-
> American coaches—including Ty Willingham (then at the
> University of Washington), Herm Edwards (then with the
> Kansas City Chiefs), and Lovie Smith of the Chicago
> Bears—expressed their support.

And, indeed, the Steelers' owning Rooney family supported
Senator Obama and even backed Democrat Ed Rendell (the former
mayor of Philadelphia) over their former star player Lynn Swann in
the race for governor of Pennsylvania. President Obama has since
appointed Dan Rooney as America's Ambassador to Ireland.

Much of Kornacky's case is rooted in the observations of men
like former Congressman Tom Osborne of Nebraska. Kornacky
writes:

> Tom Osborne, who coached the Nebraska Cornhuskers
> for 25 seasons before serving three terms in Congress as a
> Republican, suggested that football coaches probably look
> at their own lives and careers as testaments to the conser-
> vative principle of self-reliance.
> "There's an awful lot of people who want to be in coach-
> ing for the number of jobs," he said. "It's highly competi-

tive. And many of them have had to spend a fair amount of time as graduate assistants, interns—as much as four, five, six, seven, eight years—making very, very little money to get into the profession. And they will work 70, 80, 90 hours a week during the season.

"I think that background—adherence to discipline, sometimes sacrifice, loyalty to core values—those things tend to have people move in that direction."

Mr. Osborne even noted that most coaches are ex-players, joking that "I'm sure many who are more liberal would say it's because they [conservatives] got hit in the head too much."

I love that closing quote from Coach Osborne. I wish more political leaders were so sincerely and humorously self-deprecating.

Still, if anyone in government could be accused of "mushy-headedness," it would have to be those on the Left who think the federal government has the answer for how to run everything. Not only isn't that the case—which is pretty obvious to anyone with eyes to see—but the interest groups to whom liberals are beholden are often the very ones that prevent government from making common sense reforms that would benefit everyone, including our children, as we'll see in the next chapter.

CHAPTER THREE

WHAT GETS MEASURED GETS BETTER

IN THE EARLY 1960s, WHEN CAMP KEEYUMAH IN RURAL
Pennsylvania was about to hold its much-anticipated end-of-sum-
mer basketball tournament, the camp banned one of its coun-
selors from coaching. As a young camper later explained:

> Larry was so skilled at coaching even then... that in our
> most crucial intra-camp athletic competition, our end of
> the summer Color War, he wasn't allowed to coach. Having
> him on your bench was considered an unfair advantage,
> because the whole camp realized that no matter how
> much talent was stacked against him, Larry would find a
> way to win.

The young camper who grew up and penned those words, Tony Kornheiser, is one of America's most popular sports commentators today. And the counselor whose coaching genius awed Kornheiser and everyone else at Camp Keeyumah is now a nomadic basketball coaching legend, Larry Brown.

It is remarkable that Brown's unique gifts as a coach could be recognized at such a young age in such an unremarkable setting ("Keeyumah is Indian for 'child of rich parents,'" Kornheiser liked to joke). But Camp Keeyumah's sense that Larry Brown could win with almost any roster of players was certainly prescient, because Brown's professional coaching career has been distinguished by his Rumpelstiltskin-like knack for turning basketball stubble into post-season gold. Indeed, Brown has a long history of taking the NBA's bottom-feeders and fashioning them into winners, which surprised all prognosticators: Brown took a New Jersey Nets team that had won only twenty-one games in 1981 to back-to-back play-off appearances in 1982 and 1983.

He led a faltering San Antonio Spurs franchise to the biggest single-season turnaround in NBA history (thirty-five more wins) in his second year with the team.

He coached the Los Angeles Clippers for two seasons and led them to the playoffs both years—a remarkable feat given that the Clippers made the playoffs only one other time in their first twenty-seven years of existence.

Under Brown, the Indiana Pacers won an NBA playoff series for the first time, the Philadelphia 76ers made it to the NBA Finals for the first time in two decades (with a team that had won only twenty-two games the season before Brown arrived), and the Detroit Pistons won an NBA championship. Coach Brown "did it again" this season leading the Charlotte Bobcats to their first playoffs in six seasons of existence.

Between his various professional team revivals, Brown became the only UCLA coach to take the Bruins to the NCAA championship game in the first nineteen years after John Wooden retired. (Four other post-Wooden coaches tried and failed.)

And Brown won a national championship at the University of Kansas, the school's first, with a 1988 team that began the season 12–8 overall and 1–4 in the Big 8 Conference.

In all, Larry Brown is the only basketball coach ever to win both an NCAA and an NBA championship. He is one of only four coaches to win more than 1,000 NBA games. Brown has garnered national "Coach of the Year" honors at both the collegiate and professional levels. Hall of Famer Isiah Thomas, among others, called Brown the greatest "turnaround artist" in the history of coaching basketball.

"THAT ROAST BEEF IS A LOSER"

Larry Brown's success turning around losing franchises reminds me of my father. Before my dad joined the Los Angeles Rams, they had had seven consecutive losing seasons; before he joined the Washington Redskins they had come up short in fourteen of fifteen previous seasons. Like Coach Brown, part of the reason my father managed to succeed where others had failed is because he had an incredible, relentless, indefatigable will to win.

"Allen's mind is almost solely devoted to winning football games and how it can be done more efficiently," a 1970 *Sports Illustrated* profile observed. "He has written six books on the subject, and if he ever gets around to writing his Ph.D. dissertation that will undoubtedly make seven."

So consumed was my dad with winning that it permeated every part of his daily life. He kept a three-sided cardboard sign on his desk which read, "IS WHAT I AM DOING, OR ABOUT TO DO, GET-TING US CLOSER TO OUR OBJECTIVE—WINNING?"

Former NFL quarterback Roman Gabriel often told the story of the day my father walked into the Rams' break room before practice while "Gabe" was eating a roast beef sandwich.

"What are you eating?" my father asked the star quarterback.

"Roast beef," Roman replied.

"That roast beef is a loser," my father said. Motioning outdoors, he continued, "All the winners are out there—alive, walking around, eating hay."

While my father's obsession with winning amused his players at times, it also engendered their respect. Rams free safety Eddie Meador once said of my father, "He works so hard and demands that his coaches work so hard, the players feel obligated to work hard, too."

Similarly, Roman Gabriel once wrote: "I've never known a man who concentrates his energies so totally on one goal. He works day and night, weekdays and weekends, fall and spring. He fills every minute of every day with football."

My mother, Etty, often joked that the reason my dad liked ice cream so much was because he didn't have to chew ice cream—and chewing would have taken his mind off football. She also enjoyed telling a humorous story from their early courtship. On one of their first dates back in Sioux City, my mom noticed that my dad was drawing arrows, X's, and O's on his dinner napkin after the meal. "Isn't that romantic?" she thought to herself. "He must really be trying to tell me something." It wasn't until after they were married that Mom learned that arrows, X's, and O's aren't just symbols for kisses and hugs—but also for offensive and defensive players in non-romantic football plays.

Like all of us, my dad loved to win, and he *hated* to lose. One of his favorite sayings captured both sides of this coin: "Every time you lose, you die inside; but every time you win, you're reborn." Victories were exhilarating. Driving directly home after a loss was as quiet as a funeral procession.

Not surprisingly, my dad had little patience for those who could accept losing easily. He once told a reporter: "If you can accept defeat and open your pay envelope without feeling guilty, then you're stealing. Winning is the only way to go. I've heard that the average NFL player draws a salary of $25,000, but I can't think of a thing this money will buy that a loser could enjoy. Losers just look foolish in a new car or partying it up."

Lest there be any doubt, Coach Allen meant what he said. Once, after his 1983 USFL Chicago Blitz had lost to the Boston Breakers in a key game, my dad noticed that a backup quarterback was unacceptably jovial on the plane ride home. Upset by this lack of respect, my father threatened to cut the player from the roster right there on the spot. And he told the rest of the team—at 30,000 feet—"Anybody who isn't dedicated can leave *now*."

While my father was more obsessed with winning than most people, the world of sports is full of folks who would do just about anything to win. For instance, in the days leading up to Super Bowl XVIII, Redskins offensive tackle Joe Jacoby half-jokingly told a reporter, "I'd run over my own mother to win the Super Bowl." Upon hearing this, Los Angeles Raiders linebacker Matt Millen replied, "To win the Super Bowl, I'd run over Joe's mom, too."

In the realm of stock car racing, Richard Petty had his first apparent victory in a Grand National Race overturned when an ultra-competitive fellow racer formally protested the outcome of the race. Upon further review, the victory was awarded to the pro-tester—who just so happened to be Richard's father, Lee Petty!

In hindsight, this incident might not seem all that significant, since Richard Petty went on to become the "king" of stock car racing, winning 200 races—including the prestigious Daytona 500 seven times. But on the day of that first apparent win, no one knew that Richard Petty would someday win more Winston Cup championships than any other driver. Indeed, for all Lee Petty knew at the time, he could have been depriving his son of the only first place finish Richard would ever get in a NASCAR race. Yet, Lee Petty went ahead and filed his formal protest. He wanted to win—even if it meant that his son lost.

That Lee Petty story is a favorite of mine, partly because I am a long-time fan of NASCAR and Richard Petty. In fact, "King Richard" campaigned for me several times when I was running for Governor, and at a fundraiser in Danville he once offered his famous cowboy hat to anyone who would donate $5,000 to my campaign.

This Lee Petty story also makes one of my father's somewhat suspicious acts look rather trivial by comparison. Once, when the Redskins were playing at Philadelphia, the line judge made a really bad call that upset a lot of folks on the sidelines. My kid brother Bruce started hurling insults at the line judge, prompting the official to threaten an unsportsmanlike conduct penalty if "that kid" continued. Fearful of losing fifteen yards, my father quickly intervened. "That kid's not with us," Dad sought to assure the official. "He must be one of those ball boys the Eagles gave us."

No penalty was assessed.

THE IMPORTANCE OF OBJECTIVE SCOREKEEPING

The federal, state, and local officials who run our public schools could learn a lot from men like my dad and Larry Brown—from their will to win to how they turned around losing programs. Education is in many ways the great equalizer in American society.

For a person to succeed in life, the two most influential factors are family and education. Personal empowerment is derived from knowledge. The best jobs will go to those who are most prepared.

Our schoolteachers and administrators do many things well, and we should be thankful that we have so many teachers who are as dedicated to teaching students as my dad was to coaching football players. But none of us can be content with the results we're getting overall from our public schools; we should always be looking for improvement.

One of the promises I made to the people of Virginia when I ran for governor was to bring academic accountability to our schools because it was often difficult to determine which schools and which teachers were truly exceptional, and which ones were below average. Back then, no one in Virginia really "kept score" when it came to education. Oh, we measured how many fire drills were run, how many books were in the school library, and how much money was being spent. And we had some broad measurements of student achievement—things like average SAT scores and graduation rates. But these measurements came so late in students' academic life that it was hard to know where exactly a student had been helped or hurt along the way. No state, including Virginia, systematically measured classroom achievement on an ongoing basis over the course of students' progression from elementary school to middle school to high school. In fact, a passing sixth grade Literacy Passport was all that was required to graduate from high school in Virginia in 1994.

Our Administration wanted to change that, because one of the things I learned growing up around sports is that we all tend to perform better when someone is keeping score.

No one guesses the score in a basketball game. In all sports contests there are scoreboards and records. And all of us tend to "raise our game" when our performance is being regularly measured and evaluated. As George Mason University president Alan Merten once wisely expressed to me: "What gets measured gets better!"

So we launched an ambitious reform in Virginia which sought to identify which students and schools were truly excelling (and which needed to raise their performance). I named our proposals the "Champion Schools" initiative because all of us aspire for our children to attend "champion," not "mediocre," schools. With the help of 5,000 parents and educators, we established high "Standards of Learning" for each grade and then periodically evaluated student performance. With high expectations, we wanted students to jump over a hurdle rather than just a hose.

Using objective statewide tests, we were able to help students, parents, teachers, and administrators have a common benchmark to evaluate objectively how well students were learning core subjects in the classroom. (Our core subjects were reading, writing, math, science, economics, and history.) We were also able to identify areas of strength and weakness in a student's performance— and to identify students who needed more instruction rather than being "socially promoted" without having gained the knowledge and skills needed to succeed at the next grade level.

Our premise was honest and clear: Students cannot truly be "given" self-esteem. Self-esteem must be earned through accomplishments and verified achievement.

Student test scores, like sports statistics, typically tell a lot. They aren't perfect measurements, but they are extremely useful—especially in making certain that basic foundational benchmarks (or minimum standards) are reached or surpassed.

Since our Champion Schools reforms were instituted in the 1990s, the results have been outstanding. Virginia schoolchildren are learning more and performing better on state and national tests. And we are proud that our Champion Schools initiative not only became a model for other states to emulate, but that we accomplished these reforms without dictates from Washington, which, when it intrudes into education, offers pestering, bureaucratic programs that, typically, don't work, but that bribe states into compliance with federal dollars. States ought to set the standards, and I'm glad to say that more schools in more states across the country are "keeping score" to encourage excellence in the classroom.

MOST IMPROVED IS OFTEN MOST OUTSTANDING

If you ask folks to identify the best schools, they'll usually point you to the ones with the highest student test scores. Well, that's one legitimate measure. But there's another.

Most sports have Coach of the Year awards, and very often the winner of this award is not the coach whose team had the best record, but rather the coach who did the most with what he or she had. The Coach of the Year is frequently a "turnaround artist" who took a team with a history of losing and made it a winner; or a coach who battled back against the odds, keeping his team a winner despite losing key players. Rarely does the Coach of the Year award go to the coach whose team was expected to do well and did.

In coaching and teaching it's far more difficult to take a group of mediocre performers and "coach them up" to a level of excellence than it is to take a group of top performers and excel with them—though of course that's not easy either. As many a manager for the New York Yankees has found over the years, sometimes it can be very challenging to lead a group of highly paid stars and prima donnas and get them to buy into team roles and to share the spotlight with other high achievers. There's a reason baseball's Joe Torre and basketball's Phil Jackson are considered great coaches. They have a remarkable knack for getting the most out of superstar performers, and they deserve the honors and tributes that have come their way.

Still, evaluations of coaching ability typically take into account the caliber of talent one has to work with—and, increasingly, this principle needs to be applied to teachers. Specifically, in some part, teacher pay should be related to the degree of progress or improvement that a teacher helps stimulate in the classroom. As we monitor student progress we can also measure and reward teacher success. The true classroom MVPs are the teachers who are "turnaround artists," taking children who have never excelled before, leading them into personal empowerment and giving them a new sense of accomplishment, hope for the future, and greater opportunities in their lives ahead. We want to keep great schools great, but we also want progress across the board.

MERIT MATTERS

The NFL is a meritocracy. It seeks to foster and reward excellence through fair competition. While the NFL doesn't attempt to address every conceivable advantage or disadvantage that a team could encounter, it does attempt to ensure that all competition takes place on a level playing field; the rules are the same everywhere; and revenue from television and merchandise sales is shared so that teams in big media markets don't have undue advantages over teams in smaller markets.

The NFL also tries to promote parity in talent so that every team has a fair opportunity to win on any given Sunday. The NFL (like the NBA, MLB, and NHL) structures its off-season draft so that the teams with the worst records from the previous season select first from the pool of talented incoming players, while the teams that finished at the top in the previous season pick last. By following this last-shall-be-first and first-shall-be-last draft tradition, the NFL acknowledges that an even distribution of talent throughout the league fosters better competition. Every team should have an equal opportunity to succeed, though results, of course, will not be equal.

We could bring this sort of parity to our public school by tying teacher pay to student progress in the classroom, because it would encourage good teachers to go to underperforming schools and make a positive impact (for which they'd be rewarded).

Sure, there will always be "Phil Jackson" type teachers who prefer working with gifted students—we need those sorts of teachers too—and certainly, all things being equal, most teachers would rather work with well-behaved, motivated students. But all things are not equal. If teachers could earn considerably more money turning around poorly performing students at a "bad" school, then some excellent teachers, wired like Coach Larry Brown, Coach George Allen, or Bill Parcells, would eagerly tackle the challenge. And as more and more exceptional teachers went to teach at failing or inadequate schools, these newly empowered students would have a better chance of overcoming their tough background and competing for better opportunities after graduation.

I realize that teachers are not primarily motivated by pay—no one becomes a teacher to get rich. But exceptional teachers should be rewarded for excellence. In sports and the private sector, pay is based on performance. Teachers should be given the same economic incentives.

I have seen firsthand how modest economic incentives can cause a big impact in improving student performance in the classroom. In 2009, my wife Susan and I attended Jack Kemp's funeral. I considered Jack a political hero, and he had always been a great friend to me and my family. When my brother Bruce took over the head coaching job at Occidental College (where Kemp had played college ball against my father's Whittier Poets team), Jack was a big help to him. And Jack was a kindred soul and advisor to me throughout my public service. Apart from Ronald Reagan, no one in political life influenced me more than Jack Kemp. We shared a football background, a similar philosophy of government, and a desire to find and advocate innovative ideas to improve opportunities for all people.

Jack's funeral was held at the magnificent National Cathedral in the District of Columbia. Susan and I happened to sit next to the energetic, optimistic CNBC economic guru Larry Kudlow and his wife Judy. Knowing of my interest in reforming education, Judy made a point of telling me all about Cox Elementary, an inner-city school in Norfolk, Virginia, where her sister, Susan Butler, teaches. Many of the schoolchildren there were failing, in part because many of their parents appeared apathetic about their children's schooling and after-school activities.

Judy decided to do something about this lack of parental involvement. She offered to pay $10 to each parent of a child who passed a Standards of Learning test (in math, English, science, history, or economics). However, to collect the $10, a parent had to show up with her child at a school ceremony celebrating this achievement.

Judy figured that several dozen parents would take her up on her offer and help their children prepare for the tests. But she never imagined that more than 500 parents would ultimately get involved.

On the night that the $10 prizes were handed to the parents of schoolchildren passing the tests, Judy said several of the moms had tears in their eyes. Some spoke of using the prize money to take their kids to McDonald's or Burger King as a reward for the achievement. And the appreciative parents were moved by the fact that someone from outside their school cared enough about their kids to offer incentives for them to learn and succeed in the classroom.

I was so enthused by Judy Kudlow's story that I started taking notes. Then I realized I was writing on the program of Jack's funeral service. After feeling momentarily chagrined that I had defaced the beautiful, historic program, I realized that nothing would have pleased Jack more. Jack was a self-described "bleeding-heart conservative" who devoted much of his political career to developing an "empowerment agenda" that used market-based incentives to help the poor and disadvantaged reach for and achieve their potential and dreams.

My father would have approved, too. He was a big believer in providing economic incentives to reward players who performed exceptionally. As one article about his life in professional sports noted: "Allen always had the support of his players. He was not a screamer but demanded perfection. He compensated them generously, offering a wide variety of incentives—TVs, stereos, dinner for two, victory cakes from Duke Zeibert's restaurant—for outstanding play."

Not all of my dad's incentives worked as expected. Once, the Redskins' cagey veteran Ron "Dancing Bear" McDole got an incentive clause inserted into his contract that rewarded him more money for interceptions than sacks. After this, McDole uncharacteristically grabbed a few interceptions early in the season, and my father had to remind him that a defensive end's primary responsibility is to rush the passer rather than drop back into pass coverage. So, one has to be careful with incentives. But economic incentives, properly crafted, do work.

Thankfully, the idea of merit pay for teachers is beginning to catch on. A 2009 *Washington Post* article describes an effort in Prince William County, Virginia, "to offer bonuses to teachers and administrators in high-performing schools that serve poor or challenging students." This initiative, which is being driven by a former county school official named Kris Pederson, would "give good teachers an extra reason to come to tough schools or stay in them." Bonuses would be awarded according to how the schools perform on the Virginia Standard of Learning tests. According to the *Post*, Pederson's plan would reward individual teachers and the whole school as a way of fostering collaborative teamwork and school-wide spirit. "I am simply trying to put quality teachers in front of children who are at risk," Pederson says. "Those high-quality teachers might make a difference." Yes, they might—in the attitude of the students, and in their academic performance.

My father once noted in an interview: "Football isn't necessarily won by the best players. It is won by the team with the best attitude." It is the good teacher, coach, or leader who inspires people to live, learn, and work to the best of their ability. And those who help motivate young people with the greatest needs should be provided a well-deserved bonus.

THE WISDOM OF RECRUITING VETERANS

The ideas advocated to this point are:

First, schools need to measure their performance over time and across grade levels so that they can see how well they are achieving goals—and where they need help to become a Champion School.

Second, teacher pay ought to be tied to the degree of "value added" by the instructor in the pursuit of student excellence.

Third, offering economic incentives for teachers to work with underperforming students could transform opportunities in life for young people.

We come, then, to the question of which teachers (or prospective teachers) underperforming schools ought to seek out. And here, once again, let's draw upon common sense and the world of sports. Surely, readers of this book never made any "rookie mistakes." Speaking for myself, I made many mistakes in my rough and rowdy early years. I lacked something that we all need to grow into over time: maturity. Experience is, or should be, a great teacher. Boxing great Muhammad Ali once wisely observed that "the man who views the world at age fifty the same way he did at age twenty has wasted thirty years of his life."

Recognizing that experience usually helps one's performance, my father rarely relied on rookies. It wasn't that my dad disliked young, inexperienced players. It's just that he knew that tall challenges typically can be better met with an experienced team of veterans than with a group of promising upstarts still prone to making "rookie mistakes." Here's the way one magazine described my father's tendencies: "Allen always managed to woo enough savvy veterans to keep the Redskins winning. He had to. [Bill] Belichick, whose Colts started the 1975 season using a playbook identical to the Redskins'...said Allen's schemes were so complex that no rookie could have assimilated them. Allen had to get veterans."

My dad was so eager to have veterans rather than rookies that he once traded a draft pick he didn't even own for a veteran player he coveted. His group of aging veterans on the Washington Redskins were affectionately dubbed, "The Over the Hill Gang." These players were believed by their previous teams to be past their prime, but my dad and his pro player Personnel Director, the

Hall of Famer Bobby Mitchell, knew that they were "winners" who still had the mettle and the character to help the team succeed on the football field. Moreover, my dad knew that the members of The Over the Hill Gang had the kind of maturity needed to pull together in pursuit of a common goal. As one publication reported: "The Over the Hill Gang, said [John] Wilbur, has absolutely no internal problems. 'No troublemakers. No racial hang-ups. No psychological bad guys. No nothing.'"

The Ali-like wisdom of hiring experienced veterans to tackle tough challenges is just about the opposite of what our government does now to turn around underperforming schools. You've probably heard of the Teach for America program that hires bright young college graduates to teach for several years in inner-city schools in exchange for college tuition offsets. This program is noble and heartwarming and has enjoyed some success. But it is borne out of a resigned premise—that we can't attract proven great teachers to weak schools; instead we rely on the presumed enthusiasm and energy of young, inexperienced teachers.

While many of these young "rookies" show great promise (and success) in the classroom, common sense and experience tell us that we'd get better results if every school had a cadre of proven veterans, and not just veterans of the public school classroom. Retired military men and women, with twenty or more years of service, have great experience teaching young people in difficult situations—from boot camp to combat zones. And these are men and women who don't shrink from a challenge. We should make it easier—fast-track the process—for these veterans to be credentialed to teach in our public schools.

My father-in-law, Colonel Guy Larry Brown, after two tours of duty in Vietnam and twenty years of military service, retired from the Marines in the 1970s. He then started a new career teaching computer classes at Piedmont Virginia Community College (which had the first computer lab of any college in Virginia). Colonel Brown inculcated rigor, punctuality, and good humor in his students for several decades. He was a "turnaround artist," much like the better-known Larry Brown of basketball coaching fame.

THE SPECIAL JOYS OF DOING HARD THINGS

Some people might consider it a pipe dream that veterans (of the military or our public schools) would willingly take on the hard, unglamorous work of dealing with failing students in schools where discipline may have broken down. But I've seen, from my father-in-law and my father, the special joy that comes from improving the lives of students and players.

On December 19, 1989, in the twilight of my father's coaching career, he did something that stunned just about everyone in our family and in the wider world of sports. He accepted the head coaching position at Long Beach State at the ripe old age of seventy-one.

My mother threatened to start smoking again if my dad took the job. She feared that, given his driven nature, he might literally die on the sideline. My brother, Greg, who is a psychologist, offered to give Dad some free counseling sessions.

But nothing—not even the sorry state of the Long Beach State 49ers football program—could stop my dad from doing what he loved to do most in this world: coach football.

Long Beach State had nearly disbanded football in the mid-1980s due to lack of interest. The 49ers had compiled three straight losing seasons, going a combined 11 and 24. The college had no on-campus stadium, so its players had to suit up for games at the practice field locker room, ride a bus several miles to the local municipal stadium, and then play in front of home crowds less than half the size that many high school football teams attract.

"In hiring Allen, Long Beach officials said they hoped to take advantage of the coach's knack of resuscitating a program short of breath," *Los Angeles Times* reporter Gene Wojciechowski noted in a story announcing the hire.

"I didn't come here for the money," my dad stated at the news conference introducing him as the new coach. "I took this job because it was so tough, so difficult."

My dad loved the challenge of winning against the established way of thinking and defying conventional wisdom from so-called experts who say, "It can't be done." He had begun his coaching career in 1948 at Morningside College with a team that hadn't won a game in two years, making so little money that he couldn't afford a car and had to ride a bike to practice his first year. The Long Beach State coaching position took my father back to his beginnings, leading an unheralded team of unknown players that played before home crowds of fewer than 4,000 people. Some might see that as a sad end to a great career, but my father never saw it that way.

Coach George Allen was a man who loved coaching football. Whatever the level of competition, he loved to work with young men. Coaching was in his DNA. He found fulfillment in doing what he loved—even if the stage didn't seem quite big enough for someone of his stature.

Despite my mother's trepidation about her dear husband getting back into coaching, she would say later, "I realized when he went to Long Beach State that I finally understood him. The level of competition is not what matters, it's the competition itself."

The last time I was with my father was during Thanksgiving after the Long Beach season. We reviewed a column he was asked to compose for *Sports Illustrated*, in which he gave voice to my mother's sentiments. It read:

> When I took over as football coach at Long Beach State...I was told it was the most difficult job in Division I-A. The word had been that there was no money, no support, no on-campus stadium, no facilities, no hope. All of that was definitely true.
>
> We lost our opener to Clemson 59–0 on our way to an 0–3 start. Incredibly, we ended up 6–5. Only two of the 106 Division I-A teams started off 0–3 and finished with winning seasons. Alabama was the other.
>
> In my 35 years of college and pro coaching, I've experienced almost everything in football. In 1972, my Washington Redskins made it to the Super Bowl. My teams have been winners in 21 out of the 24 seasons that I have been a head coach. But the other day Billy Kilmer, who quarterbacked my Redskins, told me, "What you did at Long Beach is your best coaching achievement ever." And Dick Butkus said I hadn't lost any of my ability to prepare a team....
>
> At a time when concepts like working together and being positive seem old-fashioned to some people, I can't tell you what a reassuring feeling it is that the players—and I—showed that those ideas still have value. I learned that players need the same things they needed in 1948—discipline, organization, conditioning, motivation, togetherness, love.

It's true that my players this year needed more of all those things than athletes I'd coached in the past. They needed more attention because many of them had come up the hard way and lacked confidence. Frankly, they had plenty to lack confidence about....

We had to start all over with fundamentals. My staff and I taught stance and starts, blocking and tackling, all the things you teach a Pop Warner team. By our last game, in which we beat UNLV 29–20, my Forty-Niners were playing almost like a George Allen team....

What my staff did was to help a bunch of good guys who were drifting aimlessly. We gave them things they desperately needed as human beings. They are bigger, faster and stronger today than they were a year ago, but none of that would matter if they didn't also have character, dedication and loyalty. The other day I told my players, "Isn't it great to be a winner? I want you to put this on your resume."

[M]y players learned things this year that will stay with them for the rest of their lives.... Long Beach State president Curtis McCray told me that the difference in the players from the beginning to the end of the season, on and off the field, was "amazing."

[T]his was my most gratifying year in coaching.

Not long after he penned that article for *Sports Illustrated*, my father died of a heart athrythmia on December 31, 1990. I got the call from my brother Bruce expressing words that we find so difficult to say or hear, "Dad...has...died." We all were stunned because Coach Allen had been in such good shape. Awhile later, I remembered the time my mother had expressed to me her fear that Dad would end up dying on the Long Beach State sideline.

I had been taken aback by her comments, but I told her that Dad had to do what he enjoyed in life—coaching—and if tragedy were to strike, at least he'd go out doing what he loved to do.

That is the way my father lived his life. Coach George Allen was a "turnaround artist" who reveled in taking ragtag programs with a history of losing and turning them into winners. At the end of what he considered his most gratifying season, he died after leading a most unlikely group of players to a most improbable winning season. We should take a leaf from Coach's playbook and encourage other similarly motivated men and women to get in the game and help turn around our nation's schools.

Measure for success. Guide people to achieve to the best of their ability. And thereby improve the opportunities in life for others.

CHAPTER FOUR

DEFENSE WINS CHAMPIONSHIPS

OVER THE COURSE OF HIS 22-YEAR MAJOR LEAGUE BASEBALL career, Bill Buckner collected more base hits (but fewer home runs) than Mike Schmidt, Harmon Killebrew, and Reggie Jackson. He had a higher career batting average than Dave Winfield, Johnny Bench, and Willie Stargell. Buckner struck out less frequently than just about every member of the Baseball Hall of Fame. And he had a career fielding percentage of .991—which means that he mis-played, on average, less than one ball out of 100.

Buckner was not an all-time great. He made an All-Star team only once, and he did not receive serious consideration for the Baseball Hall of Fame.

Still, "Billy B" was a very good ballplayer for a very long time. In fact, he was so good for so long that his Boston Red Sox manager wanted to reward him by leaving him in the game for the last inning of Game 6 of the 1986 World Series. Normally, Boston skipper John McNamara put in Dave Stapleton as a late-inning defensive replacement for the aging, gimpy-kneed Buckner. But with the perpetually jinxed Red Sox on the brink of their first World Championship in nearly seventy years, McNamara decided to leave Buckner in the game so that he could be on the field to celebrate with his teammates when Boston (at long last!) won the World Series.

As every sports fan who has ever seen a baseball replay knows, McNamara's decision left Boston vulnerable. And when a routine two-out ground ball rolled through Buckner's legs allowing the winning run to score, Buckner became the iconic symbol of Red Sox futility. He became the living scapegoat onto which decades and generations of Boston baseball frustrations were thrown.

To be sure, Buckner should have made the play. And to their credit, Boston fans eventually atoned for some of the abuse—and death threats—Buckner received in the aftermath of his gaffe: they gave "Billy B" a "standing O" at the 2005 Opening Day celebration of Boston's 2004 World Championship.

It is a shame that a very good ballplayer's very good baseball career is almost obsessively associated with one very bad play. And it is an even greater shame that Bill Buckner could have been spared a lifetime of baseball infamy had his well-meaning manager remembered the first rule of hard-fought competition: *defense wins championships.*

Sadly, Buckner's Beantown manager ignored this time-honored truth. He let his guard down, forgetting an opponents' will to win until the last out. McNamara needlessly risked his team's fortunes in the last inning of the biggest game of the entire season.

Sure, McNamara's heart was in the right place. His sentiments were honorable. It would have been nice for Buckner to have been on the field to celebrate a World Championship. That would have made for a perfect storybook ending.

But McNamara never should have tempted fate. He never should have committed the mistake that many in Washington often make on issues of national security: *he never should have allowed wishful thinking to cloud his judgment.*

Many Washington policymakers today govern with an overly sentimental view of how the real world works. They imagine that our adversaries want peace every bit as much as we do. They are deluded into thinking that our enemies will respond to every good will gesture with an equal measure of good will. They believe that diplomatic platitudes will patch over virtually every international problem or dispute.

The well-meaning liberals who hold these views are right to assume that we should always prefer diplomatic solutions to military ones—but sometimes the military option is necessary. When push comes to shove, the Department of Defense matters far more than the Department of State; in fact, it's what the Pentagon does that makes the diplomatic overtures of the State Department have any hope for success at all. In foreign relations, as much as in sports, having a strong defense is what really matters.

THE RUN-AND-GUN OFFENSE

In almost all team sports, the object of the game is to outscore your opponent—and so it would seem at first blush that the key to success is to be better at scoring than your opponent.

Over the course of sports history, many teams have taken this approach. And many innovative coaches have built grand offensive juggernauts that have followed what might be called the "Paul Westhead approach" to sports success.

For the uninitiated, Paul Westhead is a former men's basketball coach who loved for his teams to "run and gun." Westhead's teams played a very entertaining, up-tempo style of basketball that put lots of fans in the stands and lots of points on the scoreboard. For example, Westhead's Denver Nuggets averaged an NBA record 119.9 points per game in 1990–1991. And Westhead's Loyola Marymount University team set similar scoring records at the college level in the late 1980s.

Nevertheless, Westhead's offensively minded teams often lost more than they won. For example, that high-scoring 1990–1991 Nuggets team won only twenty of its eighty-two games—and it set NBA records for most points allowed per game (130.8, on average) and for most points allowed *in a single half* of an NBA game (107, against the Phoenix Suns). Consequently, Westhead's almost-exclusive emphasis on offense led some critics to derisively call his team the "enver Nuggets" (because it had no "D").

The reason "run-and-gun" basketball teams often fail to compete for championships is because it's easier to defend a 20-foot jumper than to make one. It's easier to disrupt an acrobatic turnaround bank shot than to score one. And it's easier to play shutdown defense consistently than to shoot the lights out every night. Thus, over the course of a long season, teams that emphasize prolific offensive play will typically lose more games than teams that emphasize strong defensive play (because the latter don't have to "light up the scoreboard" to win).

And this isn't just the case in basketball. It's true in all sports. In baseball, many like to say that "pitching is 80 percent of the game" and that "good pitching will beat good hitting just about every time."

Similarly, in football, teams that rely too heavily on a prolific offense often end up doomed in the end. Such was the case with the Washington Redskins prior to my father's arrival in 1971. Here's how one publication described the transformation my father brought about in the Redskins' priorities:

> Upon arriving in Washington, Allen . . . said he would, as always, stress defense. The Redskins' [previous] approach to defense was to get Sonny Jurgensen to throw four touchdown passes. Against the Giants last year, Washington scored 57 points in two games and lost them both. Allen said that would not happen again. Ever.
>
> Actually, the offense didn't have to be too good because the old men on defense were brilliant. They held the Giants to three points in a very physical game. . . . After five games, a defense that had been the worst in the NFL in 1970 was now the best in the conference.

Some sports lovers only grudgingly acknowledge the importance of defense because they see low-scoring games as boring. In football, every fan is an expert on what offensive play to call, but few fans ever yell out what line stunts, blitz packages, or zone coverage schemes a defense ought to call.

Interestingly, my father saw things quite differently. He built his reputation on defense—not just by coaching his players to be tenacious defenders, but by introducing a number of innovative schemes that transformed the game. As *Sports Illustrated* noted: "Allen was one of the first coaches to employ the blitz, zone coverage and the nickel defense. . . . Since it was as a defensive strategist and teacher that Allen made his reputation, he spent most of his time during his first three years as head coach of the Rams with the defensive unit, installing what is generally regarded as the most complex system and code in pro football."

Another profile echoed this theme: "Coach Allen's heart belongs to his defense. He will often huddle with them on the sidelines, oblivious to what his offense is doing on the field. . . . Allen meets for an hour and a half after every practice with [linebacker Jack] Pardee, who is referred to by some teammates as 'the quarterback.'"

That sort of dedication to defense—and all of its intricacies and complexities—won my father much respect. In fact, one of his greatest moments in coaching came in the locker room after the 1963 NFL Championship Game when he was serving as the Chicago Bears' defensive coordinator under head coach (and owner) George "Papa Bear" Halas. Chicago had just beaten the New York Giants, 14–10 at frozen Wrigley Field. And since the Bears' attacking defense had thoroughly dominated the normally high-scoring Giants, the team presented my dad with the Game Ball, which is the most meaningful commendation any player or coach can receive from the team.

It is exceedingly rare that an assistant coach—particularly a defensive coach—is honored in this way after a championship game. But it was fitting. And it really meant a great deal to my dad and (as we will see later) to me.

PEACE THROUGH STRENGTH

The reason defensive coaches rarely get their due is the same reason that defensive players seldom get serious consideration for college football's most prestigious award, the Heisman Trophy. However important defending may be, for most fans, defense simply isn't as entertaining as offense—as can be seen on any highlight reel on ESPN. You'll see a lot more touchdown catches than defensive stops for no gain, a lot more three point baskets than baskets denied, a lot more slap-shot goals than hip checks, a lot more home runs than strikeouts. While defensive players sometimes get attention for great interceptions or "jacked-up" tackles or diving outfield catches, offensive play tends to draw far more eyeballs and receive far more glory than defensive play. And this comparative lack of appreciation for defense isn't just true in the world of sports, it's very often the case in the world of international affairs.

Want to win the Nobel Peace Prize? One is more apt to do so by negotiating a new treaty (or giving some apologetic, ear-tickling speeches) than by liberating an oppressed people overtaken by an armed aggressor.

This isn't to say that our military heroes never get any respect. We all know better. But it is to say that, oftentimes, defensive play doesn't get really noticed or appreciated unless something goes wrong—and then, suddenly, everyone is reminded of the foundational importance of a strong military. Indeed in a time of a violent threat to our country, the President's first question is often "where are our aircraft carriers?" Not "where are our diplomats?"

In sports, part of the reason defense is underappreciated is because it isn't as measurable as offense. Most football statistics, especially individual statistics, have to do with offense: plays, time of possession, rushing attempts, yards gained, completions, receptions, touchdowns.

It was "Secretary of Defense" Deacon Jones who first managed to get the "sack" recognized as an official statistic by the National Football League. His explanation for why it should be called a "sack" was pure Deacon: "You take all the offensive linemen and put them in a burlap bag, and then you take a baseball bat and beat on the bag. You're sacking them, you're bagging them. And that's what you're doing with a quarterback."

Individual defensive statistics are fairly limited—which is why Fantasy Football participants draft individual players at the "skill positions" on offense and entire units for defense. Moreover, even where individual defensive statistics do exist, sometimes a defensive player's greatness will never truly show up in the record books.

Take, for example, defensive back Deion Sanders. Over the course of his NFL career, "Neon Deion" put together an incredible highlights reel of amazing kick-off, punt, and interception returns. But he didn't rack up large numbers of interceptions. And the reason Sanders never led the league in interceptions is because other teams were so respectful of his defensive skills as a "shut down cornerback" that they rarely threw in his direction. In fact, they sometimes avoided Sanders' side of the field altogether.

What the stats won't tell you, then, is the value of Sanders' deterrent effect—the hidden effect that he had on games. Like the dog who didn't bark in the famous Sherlock Holmes story, the impact of Sanders' presence in the line-up could often be measured more by what didn't happen (passes in his direction) than by what did happen. In fact, if "Prime Time" had not received so much attention for his showboating punt returns—and his off-the-field flamboyance—Deion Sanders might never have become a household name.

In international affairs, even more than in football, deterrence is to be greatly prized. Yes, a nation must be prepared to fight a just war. It must have the will, the skill, the armaments, and the firepower to repel aggression. But the best wars are the ones that are never fought—the ones that are avoided because would-be aggressors know better than to transgress a mighty opponent that can project its power. No responsibility is more central to the proper role of government than ensuring national security. We must always have a strong, well-equipped, and well-supported military to defeat our enemies abroad and an effective defense—the FBI, state and local law enforcement—to thwart dangers on our own shores.

Ronald Reagan had many accomplishments—from revitalizing the American spirit to revving the engines of our economy. But one of Reagan's most important accomplishments was dramatically increasing our national defense capabilities to protect America and our allies, which would give our diplomacy greater clout and effectiveness. Rather than appeasing, containing, and accepting repression, it was his goal to topple the "Evil Empire," as he called it, of Soviet communism. He challenged Soviet leaders—"Mr. Gorbachev, tear down this wall," as he demanded in a speech at the Berlin Wall—and finally forced them to concede that they could not hope to compete militarily against the United States, but would have to liberalize, reform, and eventually dispense with communism. "Peace through strength" is a proven winning strategy.

My friend Riki Ellison knows well the importance of defense. Riki was a hard-hitting linebacker who won a national championship at the University of Southern California and three Super Bowl rings in the NFL.

We were having lunch together one day to discuss the Youth Impact Program, a program that helps inner city boys develop academic, athletic, and character skills to help them reach their full potential. (This program has had a positive impact on hundreds of boys in Los Angeles, Houston, New Orleans, and Tampa.)

In the midst of our lunch, I found out that during Riki's college years at USC, he studied Soviet foreign policy, arms control, and strategic defensive studies under men like William Van Cleave, the director of President Reagan's Defense Department transition team.

In these studies, Ellison saw many parallels between military strategy and football strategy. "In football, you can't win by building everything around your offense," Ellison said. "And in the real world, it's imperative that you keep the opponent from reaching your end zone, even once."

Indeed, when Ellison first learned of President Reagan's Strategic Defense Initiative (SDI), he was struck by how similar Reagan's "Star Wars" plan for intercepting incoming missiles was to some of the defensive schemes he had been a part of at USC and with the 49ers and Raiders.

"Sometimes you play zone defense, other times you play man-to-man, the key is to layer your defense so you can protect your goal line no matter how they attack you," Ellison related. "That's essentially how a missile defense system works." Ellison now heads the Missile Defense Advocacy Alliance, a national organization that promotes peace through strength. Like my friend Peter Schweizer (author of *Victory* and *Reagan's War*), Ellison recognizes that President Reagan's strategy of deterring Soviet aggression by building a strong defense helped America win the Cold War without ever firing a shot. And Ellison believes that developing and deploying an anti-ballistic-missile system is still important today, especially as rogue nations like Iran and North Korea seek to build nuclear and ballistic missile capabilities.

Riki collaborated with me to form the following football analogy to help people understand the layered missile defense system that the United States should deploy now and in the future to protect Americans and our allies.

A strong, agile defense does win championships and protects our freedom as well. Just as a good, well-balanced team needs a passing game (air force and missiles), a ground game (Army and Marines), and special teams (special forces), America must have all these forces to project our power and improve the security of our nation with the most advanced strong defense.

On defense, America must embrace innovation and adapt with a three-layered missile defense system that is fully integrated, and we must have the most current intelligence utilizing sensors.

Conceptually, sensors in satellites and band radar are akin to the whole scouting system and the communications from the press box. (Then, at 1,600 mph, we can put the bat on the ball.)

The first line of defense is the defensive line, where we need "boost phase interceptors" and early assent phase interceptors to hit missiles as they launch. These systems are like hitting a running back getting the ball. These systems can be stationary or mobile, because just like a quarterback on some offenses, we face opponents who are mobile and/or stationary.

The second line of defense (linebackers) is where we need mobile defense systems with limited range to cover slower, short-range to medium-range missiles from the opposition and tackle them after they have passed the line of scrimmage. This is called the "terminal phase layer," where the missiles enter the atmosphere on their last flight. These systems can be moved into trouble spots in the Middle East, the Korean Peninsula, or the Taiwan Straits, for example.

Third, we need "Ground-Based Interceptors" (fast defensive backs) that cover long-shot, fast, long-range missiles and bombs, which are the main threats from the Middle East, into either Europe or the United States—or from North Korea to the United States. These require tremendous speeds and pinpoint accuracy. In this game, we cannot ever allow anyone to beat us deep and score.

For the United States, we can't allow a missile in the end zone (U.S. homeland territory). We can't let the opposition score a single point, or it's "Game Over." So, we want to be able to score on them as much as possible and put the game back on their side of the field. Thus, we would force opponents to continue to punt the ball when they are on offense, or to negotiate a settlement.

The future "game changer" on defense is the Airborne Laser (ABL). It is like an outside speed rusher that can't be blocked and will hit the QB or ball carrier when he gets the ball—at the speed of light. This ABL is a transformational destructive technology which we should perfect and deploy in our American team defense.

Effective Missile Defense systems are not just interesting high-tech options for defending our nation, they are necessities.

NO OFFENSE TO THE OFFENSE

If defense is so important, how important is offense? Well, the key, as in most things, is balance. In sports, as in defending the national interest, you can't be one-dimensional.

When this happens in sports, people like Major League Baseball pitcher Ken Johnson appear, ignominiously, in the record books. In 1964, while playing for the then wonderfully named Houston Colt 45s, Johnson became the only pitcher in major league history to ever hurl a no-hitter...and lose! Johnson lost 1–0, because his team's anemic offense couldn't score a single run to match the one run its opponents manufactured without a hit.

When it happens in national affairs, the results can be equally ignominious. Jimmy Carter might be the example of a president who pledged to treat the world solely on the basis of human rights. In practice, this meant he tended not to support American allies with less than perfect human rights records, but to do little (besides boycotting the 1980 Moscow Olympics in response to the Soviet invasion of Afghanistan) to trouble our enemies who seemed to be in the ascendant while we were in decline. It also meant the disastrous fall of the Shah of Iran—the perilous results of which we still live with today—and the humiliating hostage crisis when Iranian radicals took over the U.S. embassy. When Jimmy Carter ordered a military rescue, it was a half-hearted (and again ignominious) failure. Carter believed in good intentions rather than strength—and he paid for it. We can't afford to make that mistake again. But equally, our nation's international interests can't be served solely by the military, which has a very specific function of deterring aggression and fighting wars. Still, between defense and diplomacy, defense is more important. It is no coincidence that the list of governmental functions found in the Preamble to the U.S. Constitution *begins* with "provide for the common defense."

Moreover, the founders' emphasis throughout the Constitution on providing "checks and balances" and maintaining a "separation of powers" derives from a recognition that ordinary men are capable of great transgressions, especially when they amass great power and seek to subjugate others. In our domestic affairs, defending against this means putting strict limits on the power of the Federal government; in foreign affairs it comes from being able to protect our sovereignty and deter aggression. In addition, the founders saw a need to limit the powers of the military itself, by making it accountable to elected civilian authority.

As any defensive coach knows, you don't stop an offense by being passive. So too in our national defense, our goal must be to deter aggression by making any potential aggressor understand that (a) he will fail and (b) even if he succeeds temporarily (as at Pearl Harbor or September 11), he will in the end be crushed. This no doubt helps explain interesting observations that Condoleezza Rice made to a group of NFL owners shortly after completing her service as Secretary of State. As reported in the Associated Press:

> Condoleezza Rice finally got her chance to address the NFL. Judging by the numerous standing ovations she received, Rice scored a touchdown.
>
> The Secretary of State under the Bush administration, who once aspired to be the league's commissioner, was invited by Roger Goodell to speak to the "NFL family" Sunday at the owners meetings. She spoke to several

hundred rapt listeners about everything from football to politics to the need for American optimism in a trying time.

"I am prepared to answer any questions on Russia, the Middle East, advice for the draft, the zone blitz," Rice said, drawing laughs from everyone, especially Goodell. "And why no one should ever run a prevent defense."

The reason Secretary Rice's comment that "no one should ever run a prevent defense" worked as humor is because every NFL owner, like every good national security official, knows that: *A passive, permissive defense isn't much of a defense at all.*

If America is to remain strong, we must continue to deploy effective conventional forces (to stop our adversaries' "ground game"). We must continue to develop good missile defense systems (to deter aerial attacks). And we must give increasing attention to the work of "special forces" that carry out unconventional military missions. Indeed, in our nation's current "war on terror," our maniacal, extremist, jihadist enemies do not fight "down in the trenches" like conventional forces. So, we must adjust and be prepared to deploy our special defense forces in a more effective manner than has traditionally been sufficient.

Were he still with us, my dad would no doubt appreciate the increasing importance of "special forces" in our nation's defense strategy, for as *Sports Illustrated* once noted:

Many coaches credit George Allen for being the godfather of special teams in the NFL. While with the Los Angeles Rams, Allen became the first to hire a full-time special teams coach in 1969 when he brought in Dick Vermeil. After Vermeil left in 1970 to coach at UCLA, Allen brought in Marv Levy to serve in the same role, and then many teams followed suit.

CREATING OPPORTUNITIES FOR GOOD

In one of my favorite passages from the writings of our nation's early history, John Adams wrote:

> I must study politics and war that my sons may have liberty to study mathematics and philosophy. My sons ought to study mathematics and philosophy, geography, natural history, naval architecture, navigation, commerce, and agriculture, in order to give their children a right to study painting, poetry, music, architecture, statuary, tapestry, and porcelain.

As Adams understood, all of the higher and grander pursuits of a civilization—whether in the arts, the sciences, or in commerce—depend on a stable and secure political environment that protects property and ensures artistic, innovative, and commercial freedom. Adams and other members of his generation felt that they should "study politics and war" in order to "*secure* the blessings of liberty to ourselves and our posterity."

In a sense, then, Adams was expressing what every football coach knows—that the role of the defense isn't simply to prevent the other side from causing harm, but to *create opportunities for good things to happen for others on your side*. In football, when the defense sets up the offense in good field position, it's easier for the team to score. In international politics, when the U.S. military displays appropriate power, it's easier to deter attacks from adversaries and to make them more willing to negotiate.

This is why I firmly believe that, along with advocacy of the rights to freedom of expression and religion, and the rule of law protecting privately owned property and our God-given rights, the key to scoring diplomatic points is to field a strong national defense.

Whenever I think of this principle, I am reminded of that cold wintry day back in 1963 when the Bears beat the Giants, 14–10, for the NFL Championship, and Chicago's players elected to give my dad the game ball. It wasn't just because my father had drawn up imaginative defensive schemes that held Y. A. Tittle, Frank Gifford, Del Shofner, and the rest of the Giants' prolific offense to just one touchdown. It was also because the Bears' defense—"the monsters of the Midway"—set up both Chicago touchdowns with interception returns that gave the offense the ball very near the opposing goal line. (In all, the Bears defense intercepted five passes and recovered two forced fumbles that day.)

More than thirty years after that great championship win, when I was governor of Virginia, I received a very unusual phone call. My assistant, Mary Augusta Nardo, came into my office to tell me, "There's a man on the phone named James Karlik claiming to have a '1963 NFL Champions' ring with the name 'Allen' on the side of it. He claims that he found it inside a shaving kit at the Albany, New York, airport."

It was a seemingly outlandish, surprising assertion that came completely out of the blue. I didn't know anyone named James Karlik. And I hadn't thought about this ring—or known that it was lost—in the six years since my father had passed away.

At first, we figured that this must be one of those prank calls we'd get from time to time from someone wanting to see if they could actually get the governor on the phone. But then the caller provided a telling detail. "Mr. Karlik says the ring has an engraving on the inside that says, '5 interceptions, 2 fumbles.'"

Very soon thereafter, thanks to the genuine kindness of this perfect stranger, I gained possession of my father's "1963 NFL Champions" ring. As you can imagine, that championship ring is now one of our family's most prized possessions. As my dad knew, a strong defense wins championships. More important, a strong national defense secures our country the blessings of liberty.

Top: My dad and his team at Morningside, 1948.
Below: As defensive coordinator of the Chicago Bears,
with players Richie Petitbon, Bill George, and Doug Atkins.

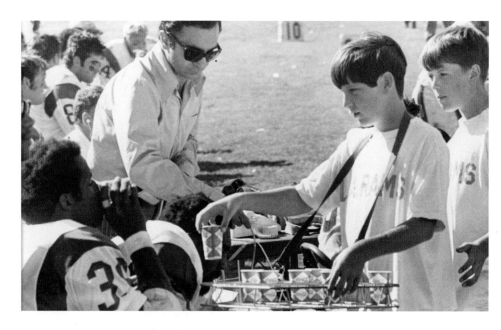

My brother Bruce, water boy for the Rams,
now general manager for the Redskins.

My dad and Governor Ronald Reagan.

President Ronald Reagan pumping iron to the delight of my father.

Dad giving a briefing to President Richard Nixon.

All for one and one for all: me, my dad, Bruce, and Greg.

Standing tall with the great Johnny Unitas.

Sharing a laugh with Billy Kilmer.

Playing rugby in Europe.

In the thrill of victory...

...and playing flag football with the old-timers.

Giving a pep talk at James Madison University.

Dad's last post—leading the team at Long Beach State.

All the Allens together at my father's induction into the Pro Football Hall of Fame in Canton, Ohio, in 2002.

Have football, will travel.

CHAPTER FIVE

NO ONE PAYS TO SEE THE OFFICIALS OFFICIATE

AT THE END OF THE 1984 REGULAR SEASON OF COLLEGE football, BYU stood alone as the nation's only undefeated team. The Cougars were ranked number one—much to the consternation of highly successful Oklahoma head coach Barry Switzer, whose second-ranked Sooners were slated to play fourth-ranked Washington in the New Year's Day Orange Bowl game.

During the month leading up to the post-season bowls, Switzer went on NBC's *Today Show*, where host Bryant Gumbel was eager to tout the Orange Bowl game between Oklahoma and Washington as a de facto national championship game (especially since NBC was broadcasting it). Gumbel questioned why BYU was ranked number one. "Who'd they play—Bo Diddley Tech?" Gumbel asked.

The always cheerful Switzer piled on. "They play in the worst conference in the country," the Oklahoma coach said. "BYU beat its schedule, but it didn't beat the world."

A number of sports columnists rushed to the Cougars' defense. "People such as Switzer keep asking: Whom did BYU beat?" wrote Tony Kornheiser in *The Washington Post*. "Hey, who beat BYU?"

Orlando Sentinel columnist Larry Guest wrote, "It's not [BYU's] fault that all the bigwig teams took the money and ran to bigger bowls, where they called press conferences to brag about how they'd bloody BYU's noses if only they could get at 'em."

In the end, BYU was vindicated. The Cougars won their Holiday Bowl game over a 6 and 5 Michigan team, and then watched on New Year's night as the Orange Bowl game between Washington and Oklahoma turned on one of the most bizarre incidents in college football history.

With the score tied at 14 in the third quarter, Oklahoma kicked a 22-yard field goal that would have put them ahead. But the Sooners were penalized 5 yards for illegal procedure on the play—and then flagged an additional 15 yards for "excessive celebration" because the Sooner Schooner, Oklahoma's famous pony-drawn covered wagon, got stuck in a patch of mud on the playing field while whooping and hollering over the apparent field goal.

After the stalled Sooner Schooner was finally removed from the field, Oklahoma attempted a 42-yard field goal—20 yards back from the original spot. The kick was blocked. Oklahoma never recovered. Washington went on to win the game, 28–17. And BYU was named national champion.

The morning after the Orange Bowl game, Baylor coach Grant Teaff teased BYU coach LaVell Edwards, "Did you hear about the big investigation going on in Miami?" Teaff asked. "Word is out that the driver of the Boomer Schooner was a Mormon."

Oklahoma coach Barry Switzer was not amused. "Washington deserves to be number one," he said in defeat. "They are 11 and 1, have the next-best record, and I guarantee you they are a better team than Brigham Young."

Needless to say, Switzer's grousing didn't go over very well in BYU's home state of Utah. In fact, the city of Midvale, Utah, passed a resolution renaming its sewage treatment center "The Barry Switzer Bowl."

"I had nothing personal against LaVell Edwards and his team—they were an excellent team," Switzer would say later. "It was my job to promote my team and promote the Orange Bowl for the national championship. I was just doing my job, and I got a sewer system named after me!"

(In 2010, a Tennessee Vols fan filed a petition to name a Lane Kiffin Sewage Center after the quickly departing coach, though there were worries that sewage would leak out and the plant would need to be replaced annually.)

Meanwhile, the latest chapter in the BYU-Oklahoma debate occurred in a direct contest. In 2009, the BYU football team had an opportunity to play Oklahoma on the field, though with different coaches at the helm—and BYU won, avenging a slight that took place before the players were born.

ANOTHER BIZARRE PENALTY, ANOTHER BREAK FOR BYU

In 2008 the Washington Huskies football team ended the season without a victory. And no episode typified Washington's snake-bitten season more than the conclusion of their second game, a 28–27 home loss to BYU.

Trailing by seven points, and with the clock running out in the fourth quarter, the Huskies marched down the field and scored on a 3-yard run by quarterback Jake Locker. In his jubilation for scoring a last-second touchdown, Locker tossed the ball over his shoulder as he jumped up to hug a Huskie teammate.

It was the kind of celebration that commonly occurs after a touchdown, especially a touchdown at such a dramatic win-or-lose moment of a game.

Or at least that's how most people saw it.

Unfortunately for Washington, one of the referees thought Locker's celebration violated the rule against tossing the ball *high* into the air after scoring a touchdown. Never mind that the rule doesn't spell out how high is too high. Or that the rule's purpose is to discourage players from delaying the game by heaving the ball into the stands. Or that Locker's "excessive celebration" did not taunt or show poor sportsmanship towards his BYU opponents.

An overzealous, nit-picky official saw an opportunity to blow the whistle. So, the Huskies were penalized 15 yards—turning their routine extra-point try into a less-certain 35-yard attempt.

As fate would have it, the kick was blocked—perhaps because longer place kicks often require lower trajectories (the kicker must kick "out" and not just "up")—and BYU won the game by a single point.

Several things need to be said about the way that 2008 Washington-BYU game ended. First, the Huskies should have converted the 35-yard point after touchdown. No, it's not a chip shot or a "gimme." But it's not a distance from which college kickers normally miss, either.

Second, there's no guarantee Washington would have won the game had the extra point been good. The point after touchdown merely would have tied the game, sending it into overtime. Given the way BYU had played throughout the day—and the fact that the Cougars were ranked number fifteen in the country—there's a fairly good chance the Huskies would have lost in overtime anyway.

Having said that, no college fan—not even a die-hard BYU loy-alist—could be truly satisfied with the ending of that 2008 game. A highly entertaining, hard-fought contest ended up mired in controversy. Rather than being decided on the field in overtime (or by a missed point after touchdown from the normal distance), everyone on both sides was left to wonder, "What if?"

What if that whistle-happy referee had remembered that college football is a *game* that's supposed to be fun to play? What if he had considered it understandable that a college kid making a big play would want to rejoice with his teammates? What if that ref had recognized that an "excessive celebration" foul should be called only when a serious delay or display of poor sportsmanship occurs?

NEEDLESSLY OFFICIOUS

Put another way, what if that nit-picky official had remembered a maxim that every self-important Washington bureaucrat needs to learn by heart: *No one pays to see the officials officiate.*

That's right, no one pays good money to see the officials officiate. No one shows up at a sporting contest hoping to see the outcome settled by umpires or officials or referees or others whose job is to govern the contest to make sure it's fair. No one expects to see contorting refs in a booth reversing a called fumble on the field into a "tuck."

Are referees needed? You bet they are. Without referees, many games would degenerate into arguments or chaos.

But the referees are not the reason folks buy tickets or watch a game on television. And however much they may want to be considered important, officials should not interject themselves into contests in ways that tilt the playing field—or the outcome—unfairly or inappropriately.

This concept is often missed by many who work in Washington. In their eagerness to "leave their mark" in government, many in Washington often impose regulations that run contrary to Thomas Jefferson's famous admonition that: *The government that governs least governs best.*

Naturally, I agree with Mr. Jefferson's sentiments. Moreover, I spent a good portion of my early life in the West and worked during hot summers on horseback on ranches near Winnemucca, Nevada, and Carey, Idaho. I like wide-open spaces, clean air driving, less restrictions, and the independent cowboy spirit of the West. As one might surmise, I don't like limits or restraints unless the activity is harming someone else.

America is, and should be, about freedom; and a basic rule in government should be that laws be kept to a minimum, because the people can and should govern themselves. There is no need for pestering, restrictive laws that set highway speed limits at fifty-five miles per hour when these highways were engineered and designed for cars to travel at eighty miles an hour. Nor is it the government's business whether you (wisely) choose to wear a seat belt while driving safely on the road. (In a speech to Western leaders in Casper, Wyoming, after hearing me blasting nanny government, State Senate leader Jim Anderson approvingly related to the audience that folks in Wyoming "don't like to use their turn signals because we don't think it's anybody's business to know where we're going.") The problem with laws is that they're meant to be enforced, which means that we have law enforcement officers wasting their time looking for people not wearing seat belts rather than focusing on serious crimes or dangerous, intoxicated drivers.

And there are larger issues where government involvement isn't just annoying but detrimental. Have you ever wondered why most Americans get their health insurance from their employer when they'd never think to ask their boss to provide them auto insurance or homeowner's insurance or renter's insurance?

The peculiar practice of having employers provide health insurance for their employees stems from an "unintended consequence" of a meddlesome federal policy adopted by officious government policymakers during World War II. Because our nation was at war and everyone was being asked to make sacrifices, someone in Washington dreamed up the idea of passing a law that would require employers to freeze workers' salaries at their existing levels.

Surely, this government-imposed "pay freeze" was well-intentioned. However, as with so many edicts that get passed in Washington, it had some effects that few, if any, anticipated. Namely, private employers responded to the federally mandated "pay freeze" by looking for other ways to compensate their employees so that they could attract and keep good workers. Some employers started offering health insurance to their employees as a way of boosting compensation without violating the terms of the government-mandated pay freeze. Others picked up the practice to remain competitive. Workers appreciated the extra compensation—especially since health insurance wasn't subject to taxation as was their regular paycheck.

And so began a practice that has now spawned all sorts of unanticipated problems—for example, people between jobs having no health insurance or workers with employer-provided insurance remaining stuck in unappealing jobs because they need the health insurance, or because someone in their family has a "pre-existing condition" that would not be covered in a new insurance policy. Employers are facing spiraling health care insurance costs partly because employees don't have the ability—or the incentive—to shop around. Competition in the health care industry isn't what it should be, which means costs are higher than they should be; and because employers have to devote so much money to health care costs, it means that workers' wages are depressed: your employer would be able to pay you a higher salary if you bought your own health insurance the way you buy your own auto insurance (and in that case, health insurance would be less costly too).

Many of the problems that now fall under the heading of "America's health care crisis" can be traced to know-it-all Washington policymakers who did *not* in fact know it all. The principles that govern every other part of our economic lives should govern health care too, because if there is one thing the free market does—besides preserve our economic freedom—we know that it provides the best quality at the lowest price. Right now we have a government-rigged system that has the disabilities of most government-rigged systems. Unfortunately, we have an administration and a Democratic Congress that think the answer to "America's health care crisis" is for government to get even more involved and issue even more dictates, mandates, taxes, and regulations and requirements, despite the fact that "socialized medicine" is not exactly a byword for quality medical care. These busybody liberals want to "leave their mark" on domestic policy. If they succeed with their expensive, massive experiment, the mark they'll leave is an exploding national debt, an arguably unconstitutional expansion of the power of the federal government over you and me, higher taxes on small business owners, and burdensome mandates on state government.

With people struggling to make ends meet, high unemployment, worries about inflation, and mountains of debt that will lead to a weaker dollar to pay the government of China and other bondholders, our federal government is on a path to spend another one trillion dollars we don't have.

Most Americans realize that this is not the time to gamble with spending a trillion dollars on a big government health care experiment. Rather than forcing dependence on government, officials in Washington should empower individuals, families, and small business owners to control their own destiny. While President John F. Kennedy famously said, "Ask not what your country can do for you, ask what you can do for your country," the rejoinder should be, "Ask what you can do for your family and yourself" with empowering policies. This is the essence of the constant contentious battle between government controls versus individual freedom.

The government should keep their hands off our health care decisions and choices. Washington's official leadership is so disconnected from the people and positive foundational principles that they appear as clueless as a hog looking at a Timex watch. With very few empowering ideas or real solutions emanating from officials' locker rooms in Washington, the most coherent health care reform proposal comes from a person outside of government. John Mackey, the CEO of Whole Foods (and no relation to the former Baltimore Colts great of the same name), has been promoting the best comprehensive ideas for reform that would significantly lower the cost of quality health care for all Americans. Mr. Mackey believes, as I do, and as I have long advocated in government and now in practice as a private citizen, in Medical or Health Savings Accounts, which allow you to put money away tax free for use on health or medical needs.

Money in Health Savings Accounts (HSAs) that isn't spent in one year rolls over to the next, and after several years grows into a good nest egg. When you're saving money for your own health care, you're much more conscious of getting value for your money—instead of just accepting whatever your employer has to offer. It's an incentive that, if it became the dominant means of financing health care, would revolutionize the health care industry in the way that most of us want to see: the best care at the best price, with you in charge.

The ideal should be to lift the barriers—including tax barriers—that discourage Americans from owning their own health insurance policies. What we need is not more government mandates, but more freedom to buy the insurance that's right for you, your family, and your budget, and that you can take with you from job to job, without any worry about your next employer or about having to apply for new insurance with "pre-existing conditions" (because you would have had insurance for years).

My point is that the central government officials need to get out of the way and let Americans make their own choices with individually owned, portable, less expensive, less bureaucratic, higher quality health insurance.

MAKE-UP CALLS

As the health insurance example illustrates, once officialdom in Washington starts down the path of excessive government intervention, it isn't easy to turn back. Like referees who follow up a bad call with a "make up call" that is every bit as suspect, Washington policymakers often follow manipulative government schemes with equally suspect counter-balancing measures—which is how we get a federal tax code that is so ridiculously voluminous and excruciatingly confusing that it has become increasingly difficult for Internal Revenue Service auditors to determine whether inaccuracies on federal tax forms represent a deliberate attempt to cheat on one's taxes or a simple (and understandable) failure to divine or comprehend what the IRS requires.

Over the last quarter-century, the U.S. tax code has grown exponentially, as all sorts of new provisions have been added. Often, these new provisions are variations of a previously adopted idea. So, we now have several different tax credits and deductions that seek to offset college education costs and several different tax-favored retirement savings plans, to cite but two examples.

Considered in isolation, there is usually some compelling reason for why this tax provision or that tax measure is adopted. Nonetheless, the cumulative effect of all these special tax measures is very burdensome, confusing, and counter-productive.

According to the National Taxpayer's Union (NTU), complying with the nation's Tax Code now costs American families and businesses more time, money, and frustration than ever in our history. In a recent study of tax complexity trends, NTU found that there are now three times as many pages of instructions for filing a federal 1040 "long form" as existed in 1985, the year before federal tax forms were last "simplified." In addition, the supposedly simple 1040 "short form" now has an instruction guide that is as long as the one for the "long form" in 1985. And the total amount of time needed for all U.S. taxpayers to fill out all federal tax forms now comes to nearly eight billion hours a year!

The IRS reports that at least 80 percent of all taxpayers now require some help in filing and paying their taxes. And that help doesn't come cheap. The National Taxpayers Union estimates that Americans spend (or waste) 300 billion dollars a year on tax compliance. Some of this cost is in direct out-of-pocket expenditures to pay the tax preparers at H & R Block, CPAs, or to buy the current software version of Intuit or Turbo Tax. Some of this cost is in opportunity costs in lost time to do other productive work. And while just over half of all tax compliance expenditures are paid by corporations, there is little consolation in this fact, because these expenditures are generally passed along to others—which is another way of saying that when businesses have to shell out big bucks to comply with complex tax laws, consumers ultimately pay higher prices, employees end up with lower pay increases, and shareholders receive smaller dividends.

It is painfully clear to most of us that federal income tax regulations are far too complex. Worse, as Steven Malanga, a senior fellow at the Manhattan Institute, points out, America's tax code is getting ever more complex, while many other countries have learned the virtues of simplicity. Malanga writes:

> A survey of the 30 member nations of the Organisation for Economic Co-Operation and Development found that most enacted some type of simplification of their tax systems in the current decade. We haven't simplified ours in 23 years. That's one reason why another study ranked the U.S. as 122nd in tax complexity out of 175 nations.
>
> Most countries opt for simplification by flattening out their tax code, that is, by reducing the number of tax rates and eliminating most, if not all deductions and credits, so that it's much easier to figure out your taxable income. Reforms of this sort also involve lowering tax rates because the new code exposes much more income to taxation.

And Malanga doesn't see our predicament changing for the better anytime soon:

> It's only going to get worse in the near-term. The first Obama budget makes a series of adjustments to the code that the administration claims will make our system fairer, but at the price of even more complexity. Nothing is more

illustrative of the problem than Obama's proposal to reduce the value of the deduction for charitable contributions made by those in the top tax bracket, whom the administration argues benefit disproportionately from their giving. To do this the government must add yet another calculation to the process of determining a tax bill which treats charitable donations at a different rate from a filer's other deductions. If something as benign as charitable donations gets this treatment, you can be sure that many other deductions will soon be similarly indexed. The potential for slicing and dicing the system when you think this way is never ending, so that soon every deduction may have its own rate schedule.

Simply said, the current federal tax code is so complicated that most ordinary people find it impossible to navigate. As with so many practices in Washington, it doesn't have to be this way.

For years, I have joined with other tax reform advocates in supporting a variety of Flat Tax proposals that would reduce the entire federal tax form to a single post card. While I have argued that the federal government shouldn't require all taxpayers to use it—because it would be unfair to change the rules on people who have made economic investment decisions based on current tax law and would prefer to stick with the existing system—I am convinced that most taxpayers would find a Flat Tax fairer and easier to navigate than current law. And lower- and middle-income working people would especially benefit from a tax simplification reform of this kind. As Malanga notes:

[T]he cost of increasing complexity falls heaviest on the lowest-income filers. A 2001 study by the Tax Foundation estimated that individuals who earn under $20,000 annually spend the largest percentage of their income on preparation and compliance of any group—an average of 4% at the time of the study.

Another problem with complexity is the cost of unintended consequences in a system where change is so common. Exhibit A is the Alternative Minimum Tax, enacted in 1969 to target 155 high-income filers whom news reports said were benefiting from huge deductions. The original AMT raised just $122 million in income (the equivalent of $671 million today) by capping the value of certain deductions, according to the Tax Policy Center. But because the AMT was not indexed to inflation and has progressively applied to more and more taxpayers, some 3.8 million filers now must pay it, to the tune of $30 billion. In two years, that sum is projected to rise to $100 billion. The AMT has grown so large that Washington can no longer afford simply to repeal it, even though it was never designed to operate as it now does.

Faced with this mess, we can derive many benefits from simplification: It would produce savings for most Americans without an actual tax cut. The largest gains would accrue to lower-income filers. Simplification would cut down on mistakes by filers and make IRS audits much simpler.

In a discussion a few years ago with my friend and fellow hockey fan, economist Stephen Moore (now with the *Wall Street Journal*) shared a great idea that actually was first conceived many years ago in Hong Kong. Steve Moore calls this tax reform approach "The Freedom to Choose Flat Tax."

I like this option because it would give us, the taxpayers, the opportunity to "opt out" of the convoluted, expensive, stressful, time-consuming preparation associated with the current tax code. Instead, a taxpayer could pay a combined federal payroll and income tax of 25 percent of gross income.

There are many of us who like the tax deductions for interest on home mortgages, employer-paid health care, and so on. Those who like the current system would be able to stay in it.

But there are many Americans who might find the "post card" alternative tax return of only four lines attractive. In Hong Kong, once one chooses the 25 percent flat tax option one "cannot migrate back into the old system." Over time, the old, convoluted tax system in Hong Kong has been "rendered obsolete" with the flat tax option.

With so much of our debt held by vibrant Asian economies, we can't afford to weigh our economy down with a tax code that taxes our patience, our time, and our efficiency as well as our wealth.

STIFLING "FLOW"

One neglected aspect of government over-regulation is that it hinders "flow."

That is, in the same way that referees who call every last ticky-tack foul disrupt the essential flow of the game, government policymakers who over-regulate human affairs disrupt the creative "flow" of commerce and ingenuity that is at the heart of America's greatness.

One of the most principled founders of our country, George Mason, warned English merchants prior to our secession from the British monarchy that "There is a passion to the mind of man, especially a free man, which renders him impatient of a restraint."

And, in his provocative book, *Flow*, Mihaly Csikszentmihalyi describes the sense of creative exhilaration and fulfillment that people experience in those rare moments when they are performing at the very height of their creative abilities. Think of what it means for LeBron James or Michael Jordan to have a "hot hand" or to be "in the zone"—where everything they throw at the basket goes in. That's flow.

And this elusive state of human flourishing exists somewhere between what Czikszentmihalyi calls the zone of anxiety and the zone of boredom. As Czikszentmihalyi notes in describing his research: "[E]very flow activity, whether it involved competition, chance, or any other dimension of experience, had this in common: It provided a sense of discovery, a creative feeling of transporting the person into a new reality. It pushed the person to higher levels of performance...."

America, with its free economy, has had remarkable success finding that sweet spot between risk and reward. But we're in danger of losing it. Nothing kills the "flow" of our economy—and all the benefits it brings in creativity, innovation, wealth, and self-fulfillment—more than a government that creates ever more complex and burdensome regulations and taxes.

As Peggy Noonan wrote in a poignant essay in *The Wall Street Journal* (October 29, 2009), business executives are becoming so depressed by the taxes and regulations coming from Washington's power elite that many of them are ready to pack it in. One executive told her that the people in Washington "don't understand that people can just stop, get out. I have friends and colleagues who've said to me, 'I'm done.' He spoke of his own increasing tax burden and said, 'They don't understand that if they start to tax me so that I'm paying 60%, 55%, I'll stop.'" Noonan noted that this insurance company executive was particularly exercised by Congressman

Barney Frank's pledge to increase regulation on that industry. The executive, she wrote, "felt government doesn't understand that business in America is run by people, by human beings. Mr. Frank must believe America is populated by high-achieving robots who will obey whatever command he and his friends issue. But of course they're human, and they can become disheartened. They can pack it in, go elsewhere, quit what used to be called the rat race and might as well be called that again since the government seems to think we're all rats."

That's what happens when the refs think the game belongs to them rather than to the coaches and players—or when government thinks that it, rather than the American people in their own independent decisions as producers and consumers, runs the economy. Of course it is discouraging if every other play draws a penalty, if the rules are constantly changing, if the government keeps moving the goal posts, or enlarging or shrinking the strike zone, or changing what constitutes a foul. There can be no flow, no sense of accomplishment, when the officials (or the bureaucrats) decide it is their role to determine every outcome. That's not how it is in sports—and that's not how it should be in our free economy. America is and should be about opportunity and hard work—that's what has traditionally made America a dynamic and optimistic country. We are in danger of losing that adventurous spirit the more government takes over our responsibilities and decides to make us all dependent on the whims of congressmen and bureaucrats.

Moreover, over-regulating burdens imposed on American vitality places our country at competitive disadvantage compared to the growing economies elsewhere in the world.

The United States can no longer afford to make mistakes. When President Reagan came into office, Americans were enduring higher unemployment, higher inflation, and much higher interest rates. Reagan's policies revived America. However, in the 1980s our competitors were Japan and Western European countries. These days, our competition is Japan and all of Europe, as well as South Korea, China, Malaysia, Indonesia, Singapore, India, Brazil, and other growing countries. America can no longer bumble in the pits while other countries are growing and racing with the pedal to the metal.

YOUR ATTITUDE DETERMINES YOUR ALTITUDE

Much of Noonan's essay focuses on how low morale leads to low performance. That resonates with people, because we all understand the importance of team spirit.

"The way to win," my father once told a reporter, "is to get good athletes, get them in shape, and have great morale." My dad was always looking for players who loved the game of football and played it with a child-like joy and enthusiasm. This is no doubt why he encouraged so much fun-loving activity on his teams. And why so many players loved playing for him.

"He was the ultimate player's coach," former Redskin captain Brig Owens once said of Coach Allen. "But at the same time he was a quiet disciplinarian. He never embarrassed you. He'd take you aside, but you got the point. You couldn't make mistakes. When the bell rang, he expected you to perform. And we did things I couldn't imagine any other players doing."

Long before the NFL came to be known as the "No Fun League" (for routinely penalizing "excessive celebrations"), my dad coached some of the most fun-loving teams that pro sports has ever known. And their enjoyment of the game—and of each other—was part of the secret to their success. As one 1970s *Sports Illustrated* profile on the Redskins observed:

> This year's Redskins are undoubtedly the sunniest collection of grizzled veterans, former player reps, reputed problem children and Men Who Have Played Out Their Options in the whole U.S.A. If there is anyone among them who does not know how to have a good time it is not George Allen's fault. "The players around here are happy because they're treated like men," says Assistant Coach Joe Sullivan. "They are responsible for their actions. But you have to be part kid to play. It's a contact sport. It takes exuberance. We treat them like men while recognizing that they're kids."
>
> In the dressing room after each victory Allen leads his adult minors in three cheers for themselves.... On the plane home from away games the players sing. They call Allen "Ice Cream," and the words to one of their favorite numbers are "Hooray for Ice Cream, Hooray at last, Hooray for Ice Cream, He's a horse's ass." Allen just smiles benignly upon the choral group. If the players like something, Allen thinks it's great.
>
> They call him Ice Cream because he adores the stuff and because that's what he gives them every Thursday after a win. Duke Zeibert, the well-known Washington restaurateur, brings ice cream and cake out to practice, and all those hardened, bleeding, bull-sized professionals line up like little tads at a birthday party.

It would be a mistake to believe that all of my dad's fun-loving positive motivational tactics worked the way he intended. In fact, once, prior to a USFL playoff game, my dad brought a mouse and a boa constrictor into the locker room because his team was getting ready to play the high-powered Houston Gamblers, led by the strong arm of future Hall of Fame quarterback Jim Kelly, and most ably coached by "Mouse" Davis.

The idea was to have the snake eat the mouse as a way of foreshadowing what my dad's Arizona Wranglers team was going to do to Mouse's "Run and Shoot" offense. But the snake didn't cooperate. In fact, after the mouse starting nibbling at the boa's nose, the snake wanted no part of it at all. Finally, my dad got so frustrated that he told the team, "Aaah, that snake's a loser" and he ordered them to get it out of his sight. Then, the Wranglers went out and won the game anyway on defense and special teams.

So, not every motivational tactic worked the way dad intended. But he would fully understand what Noonan was saying. He would fully understand the perils of having officious regulators get in the way of the main event.

Excessive government regulation thwarts commerce, hinders innovation and risk-taking, inhibits investment, stifles creativity and economic growth, and limits our freedom, while spawning dependency, dampening enthusiasm, diminishing personal responsibility, and preventing the productive exhilaration that comes with "flow."

In his classic work, *Democracy in America*, Alexis de Tocqueville marveled at the creative energy he found in America in 1835. He wrote: "America is a land of wonders, in which everything is in constant motion and every change seems an improvement. No natural boundary seems to be set to the efforts of man; and in his eyes what is not yet done is only what he has not attempted to do."

For America to continue to ascend, that must remain the essence of the enterprising spirit of America. We should only be limited by our own imagination, diligence, and ingenuity. We can't let an officious government bureaucracy take away our full potential to compete and succeed.

CHAPTER SIX

NEVER PUNT
ON FIRST DOWN

WHEN THE FLORIDA STATE FOOTBALL TEAM PLAYED AN
early-season game against Clemson in 1988, the Seminoles
showed up with something to prove.

Clemson, after all, owned the only national championship
either college had ever won (up to that point). The Clemson Tigers
were the two-time defending ACC champs and the third-ranked
team in the country. They had a sellout crowd of more than 75,000
ardent, vociferous fans cheering them on at Clemson's Memorial
Stadium—popularly known as Death Valley.

Florida State's head football coach, Bobby Bowden, would
become one of the winningest football coaches in college football
history; and on that September day, Bowden made the single
greatest play call of his career.

With the score tied at 21–21, and only 1:33 remaining in the contest, the Seminoles faced a fourth and four on their own 21-yard line. Bowden sent out the punt team, prompting the Clemson faithful to rise in exultation, imagining that even if their star punt returner Donnell Woolford had to call for a fair catch, the Tigers would still take over possession around midfield with enough time to score a game-winning field goal or touchdown.

In reality, Florida State had no intention of punting the ball. Bowden had called a trick play—known as "puntrooski"—which the Seminoles had been saving for such a circumstance. Though they had practiced it often, the play represented a huge gamble. If it failed, Clemson would take over deep in FSU territory and would almost surely win the game.

FSU snapped the ball to fullback Dayne Williams, who snuck the ball to upback LeRoy Butler, and then took off to the right side acting as if he still had the ball. Meanwhile, punter Tim Corlew faked as if the snap had gone flying over his head. Some of the Clemson players raced toward Corlew looking for a loose ball; others sought to tackle Williams running right. Butler stood in place for a split second and then took off running up the left sideline with the ball. He sped untouched for more than seventy yards before being stopped by Woolford short of the Clemson goal line. From there, the Seminoles ran down the clock, and then kicked a last-second 19-yard field goal to win the game, 24–21.

BRUCE FAKES OUT BOWDEN'S TEAM

Part of the reason I love this story is my great respect and admiration for coaches like Bobby Bowden who are willing to put it all on the line to win, even if it means calling a fake punt on fourth-and-four from your own 21 with the score tied and less than two minutes to go in the game. (During my playing days at the

University of Virginia, we were on the losing end of several games against Bobby Bowden's outstanding West Virginia teams.)

But the other reason I love this story is because any time anyone mentions "Bobby Bowden" and "fake punt" in the same sentence, it reminds me of another play from another season in a game involving my brother, Bruce, who punted for the University of Richmond Spiders against Bobby Bowden in his last year as coach of the West Virginia Mountaineers.

My brother was not just a punter—he was a football player. That is, he wasn't one of those punters who never gets his uniform dirty, who can't tackle, or who wears a wristwatch on the field. (In 2008, New Orleans place kicker Martin Gramatica missed a field goal because he was distracted by the wristwatch worn by his holder, who was a punter.)

The night before the game, Bruce let me in on a secret: the Spiders had been practicing a fake punt play they intended to run against WVU. The Spiders' long snapper would hike the ball to Bruce, who would hold the ball in one hand behind his back while going through the motions of punting the ball. If all went as planned, the rushers would see Bruce's leg in the air or see him facing his blockers as if he'd just punted the ball, and then turn tail and go running back to block for their return man. When they did that, Bruce would sprint downfield. If, however, West Virginia's rushers weren't fooled, Bruce would get the snot knocked out of him. In that 1975 game in Richmond, the Spiders' fake punt worked to perfection. Bruce ran to the 1-yard line before he got clobbered by a Mountaineer defender.

AN ADMISSION OF FAILURE

As much as I like Bowden's puntrooski call, and the fact that my brother wasn't one of those wristwatch-wearing punters, it still needs to be said that no team ever looks forward to punting in American football. (In Canada, a team can score one point—a "rouge"—on a punt). No team ever wants to face a fourth down where the only logical choice is to give the ball to the other team.

Sure, there are times when punting is safer than the alternative of giving up field position; and it can be used to pin an opponent back near his own goal line (on a "coffin corner" punt)—but still, punting is a sign—an admission—that the offense couldn't "matriculate the ball down the field" as Coach Hank Stram would say. So, no team ever enters a game hoping to punt a lot, because punting represents the failure to score.

That a team should punt only as a last resort seems obvious to anyone who has ever played or watched the game of football. And it ought to be obvious to policymakers in Washington. Yet, all too often, many folks in Washington approach serious national challenges with a punt-first mentality.

Ronald Reagan, who visited L.A. Rams' practices during his days as Governor of California, was very mindful of this tendency. As best-selling author Peter Schweizer has noted: "During the Cold War, Ronald Reagan criticized the policy of 'containment' toward the Soviet Union on the grounds that it was defensive and reactive and not designed to win the superpower competition. As the Gipper described it, the strategy was a little like playing football, and then, when you get the ball—punting on first down."

During my time in the U.S. Senate, I saw this tendency to avoid taking initiative. Washington tends to attract many friendly, articulate, and experienced folks who are all too happy simply to pontificate about problems rather than take the often difficult steps needed to actually solve them. More than ever, each senator's vote is pivotal for good or bad proposals. However, most politicians appear content to kick the can down the road and leave someone else to deal with the tough decisions.

THE FUTURE IS NOW

But the reality is, the future is now. We can't afford to kick the can down the road, because we are facing dire consequences if we do. Our country's debt has exploded, we're losing jobs, and we're in danger of losing our competitive edge in world trade. These are problems that are not going to be solved by ignoring them, or tying up our economy in more red tape, or by more wasteful and counterproductive "stimulus" programs that only put us deeper in debt, or by raising taxes—though we know that's what government loves to do.

Many Americans today are so frustrated with their government because they do not see Washington policymakers approaching some of our nation's most serious problems—like jobs and the economy—with the same sense of urgency average citizens take to their businesses every day.

The owners of the government, the people, see the distant federal government as disconnected from the concerns that people discuss at their kitchen tables. In a sense, people look at the federal spending binge as if the gluttonous Mr. Creosote has arrived uninvited for supper.

My modern political hero, Ronald Reagan, once observed that "government's view of the economy could be summed up in a few, short phrases. If it moves, tax it. If it keeps moving, regulate it. If it stops moving, subsidize it." Today, Washington has an expanded view of the economy: If it's big and failing, invest in it. If it's a government program, expand it.

No one likes to see a financial institution, auto manufacturer, or any business fail. It is heartbreaking to see people lose good-paying jobs, whether in Virginia, Michigan, Missouri, or South Carolina. But our government was not created to be the lender or stock purchaser of last resort for failing businesses. Taxpayers have their own bills to pay. And it does no good to burden our economy with more taxes, regulation, government spending, and mountains of debt. All these knee-jerk Washington reactions are part of the problem, not part of the cure.

What we need is credible reining in of government, a lowering of taxes, and a slashing of costly, bureaucratic regulations so that business owners have confidence to hire new employees, entrepreneurs are freer to innovate and launch new businesses, and our country can better compete in the global economy.

Thanks to rampant spending, the annual federal deficit tripled in 2009. And the total federal debt is projected to double in five years and triple in ten years. Future generations are being loaded with perpetual debt. That's not just immoral—shoving all that debt onto our children and grandchildren—it is dangerous, weakening the dollar and putting us in hock to foreign investors, including China.

Our government should be like a good sports team—soberly focused on specific responsibilities, not meddling in the people's affairs, and spending on someone else's credit card like a bloated, drunken nanny.

REAGAN'S TWO...AND ONE

Just as there are rule changes in sports—like the shot clock in basketball—that improve the action, there are government reforms that could improve our future. One such reform is a Taxpayer's Bill of Rights—a necessary reform that would lessen the debt burden being imposed on current and future generations of Americans.

We need to remember: we have a huge deficit not because the federal government taxes too little, but because it spends too much.

In his farewell address to the American people, Ronald Reagan said there were two things he wished he had had as president (and that he hoped future presidents—both Republican and Democrat—would obtain): the line-item veto and a constitutional amendment to balance the federal budget.

Reagan was right about the line-item veto, and I know that from experience. As Governor of Virginia, I had the line-item veto—as do forty-three governors throughout the country. I know it's a powerful tool to cut wasteful spending and undesirable or non-essential programs.

In Washington, a president has to sign big appropriations bills, which contain mostly important spending, but often include unnecessary spending items like "Bridges to Nowhere." To get rid of these wasteful extras, the president currently is stuck with vetoing a whole appropriations bill that is usually several months late. Either that, or he can sign the bill despite its wasteful spending provisions.

The President of the United States should have the same power as most governors. A constitutional amendment to provide the president with line-item veto authority is needed more than ever with all the "stimulus" spending in vogue in Washington.

Like President Reagan, I also believe we need a constitutional amendment that will require Congress and the President to balance the budget.

Balancing the budget is not just a matter of making sure that expenditures are equal to revenue; it's about making sure the federal government fulfills its proper, constitutional role—and is not expanding into everything, including matters reserved to the people or the states. One of the best ways to limit the size and scope of the government is to wrestle it down with the chains of the Constitution. Granted, the Federal government has managed to wriggle free from some of the constraints of the Tenth Amendment, but a balanced budget amendment would help redress the balance.

I have a third idea to add to Reagan's two. It won't be popular in the halls of Congress, but it will be much appreciated by the rest of us. What I propose is a powerful incentive for Senators and Representatives to perform their jobs on time, just like people in the private sector. It is absurd that full-time legislators can't get their job done by October 1 (the beginning of the fiscal year when appropriations are to be determined). Instead, usually, there are so-called "continuing resolutions" until just before Christmas. These resolutions allow Congress to pack loads of unscrutinized spending into voluminous "omnibus" spending bills that they send to the president.

That's why we should impose on Congress a "paycheck penalty." It would say to Members of Congress, "If you fail to pass all appropriations measures by the start of the fiscal year—which is your job and what you are paid to do—then your paycheck will be withheld until you complete your job." This is what happens in the real world—if a contractor doesn't finish his work on time, his paycheck is withheld until the job is done.

We need to get back to basics. A line-item veto, a balanced budget amendment, and a paycheck penalty would finally restore some fiscal accountability and common sense to Washington.

PUNTING ON ENERGY

Washington policymakers have been punting on energy for decades. Going all the way back to the 1970s, when the OPEC cartel began manipulating worldwide oil prices by severely restricting oil exports, U.S. policymakers have known that America's increasingly heavy dependence on foreign oil makes our economy vulnerable to outside forces. Moreover, Americans are disgusted that we continue to be jerked around by oil-wealthy dictators, oligarchs, and cartels.

Yet, many in Washington have been reluctant to tackle this challenge because the best alternatives to foreign oil have powerful political constituencies arrayed against them. It doesn't seem to matter that this issue is vital for American jobs, our competitiveness, our balance of trade (41 percent of our trade deficit is due to foreign oil), and our national security. Energy is also vital to American families who pay the price in high electricity, fuel, and food bills.

Notwithstanding what some pompous elites say, Americans are *not* addicted to oil. Americans are addicted to freedom—the freedom and independence to go where we want, when we want. And we should keep that freedom. We don't care whether our vehicles run on Louisiana or Alaska oil, Wyoming coal synfuels, re-used cooking oil, Texas natural gas, or nano-tech enhanced batteries— so long as it's available, reliable, and affordable.

Americans want—and deserve—affordable, reliable, and clean American Energy. We have the energy resources we need under our land and water. We have the resources in our creative people. What's stopping us then? Washington, which would rather punt on energy than handoff America's energy resources to the American people and let us run with them.

Electricity is the lifeblood of our homes and businesses, but America, the most powerful nation on earth, is running out of power. Our demand for power is going up, but we're not generating enough new power to meet demand. According to the most recent North American Reliability Study, the demand for electricity in the next ten years will grow by 17 percent while our electricity generating capacity will grow by only 6 percent.

Our economy is more dependent on electricity than ever. We're in the age of the Internet, computers, Blackberries, and iPhones; of microwave ovens, electric clocks, and electric pumps; of electronic heating and cooling, refrigeration, and lighting. Records—medical, financial, personal, business—are all stored electronically in large data storage centers, which use as much electricity as a city of 34,000. Our means of communications—television, radio, and increasingly even newspapers—are all electronic. That demand is only going to increase, and we need to have the energy capacity to keep it going with no sags, surges, or disruptions.

The two most available sources for base load electricity are coal and nuclear power. Hydroelectric power is as affordable as coal, but most of the rivers that can be used for hydroelectric power are already being used (they're mostly in the West), and their use is controversial because it requires damming the rivers. Unlike hydroelectric power, coal and nuclear power can be delivered anywhere. Already coal fuels half of our electricity. One reason most Americans have not felt the same financial pain at the light switch as they have at the gas pump is that coal is relatively affordable; that will change if more costly natural gas is used as a base-load source.

Don't get me wrong. Natural gas is a great, relatively clean-burning fuel, but to use it for base-load electricity is like using bottled water to wash your dishes. It would do the job, but why use such an expensive, valuable source when others are available? Historically, coal is one-third to one-fourth the cost of natural gas.

As more natural gas is used for electricity, including as the backup fuel source for intermittent wind and solar power, the price of natural gas will rise, and it will divert natural gas from where it really needs to be used—in manufacturing. Manufacturers of plastics, fertilizer, chemicals, tires, glass, and forestry products use a great deal of natural gas. As an illustration of this predicament, the

National Association of Manufacturers has reported that the United States has already lost more than 300,000 jobs in the chemical and paper industries because of the relatively high price of natural gas in our country.

There are some who say the importation of liquefied natural gas (LNG) is a solution. If Washington discourages the use of American coal and prevents access to newly discovered natural gas reserves under our land and off our coasts (both unproductive policies favored by many liberals), then Americans could become reliant on imported LNG. But if we want strategic American energy independence, the last thing we need is to become vulnerable to another energy cartel—specifically the recently formed LNG cartel among Russia, Iran, Qatar, and Venezuela.

The most commonly mentioned alternatives to petroleum for running our cars and trucks are natural gas and batteries. (Liquefied coal is another option, but is more likely to be used for aviation fuels.) Natural gas is feasible for school buses and delivery fleets which return to the same location and pump up every day. But for most of our ground transportation, the best alternatives are hybrids or battery plug-ins that can be recharged anywhere there is an electrical outlet—and that underlines the fact that what we really need are more efficient, cost-effective ways of producing and delivering more and more electricity.

A WINNING ENERGY GAME PLAN

With the urgency of a two-minute drill, down by six points with no more timeouts, there are five achievable goals we need to pursue for a brighter energy future.

First, we must embrace common-sense conservation and operational strategies that will save energy and money; and government ought to lead the way. We waste too much electricity, fuel, food, and water. Technological advancements, especially in nanotechnology, can improve battery capabilities and help make vehicle materials lighter and stronger, thus requiring less energy for propulsion. There are also endless innovative systems, equipment, roof treatments, and designs for better office buildings, manufacturing plants, and homes, which can conserve water, power, and other resources. Government has a role to play here—not in the sense of imposing costly regulations on businesses, but in its own operations.

When government building designers are deciding to invest in new and possibly more expensive energy-efficient systems or construction, they should consider the "life cycle" costs of the newest innovations. If the new construction or retrofitting of a building can "break even" in energy or water costs in seven years, that makes economic sense. We know that school and college buildings, courthouses, hospitals, prisons, and government office buildings will be in use for at least 50 to 100 years. If it costs less to heat, cool, and illuminate a building, then it sure makes sense to save taxpayers money by operating their government more efficiently over the long-term life cycle of the system. Similarly, it makes sense for government-owned ground transportation to be focused on hybrid cars, or vehicles with nanotech-improved batteries, and to keep these improved vehicles in service long enough to recoup any additional costs. That's step one.

Second, we ought to encourage technologies that enable coal to continue generating clean, affordable electricity while providing hundreds of thousands of American jobs. We have far more reserves of energy in our coal than Saudi Arabia has in its oil. America has more energy resources than any other country; and a big part of that is our 27 percent of the world's supply of coal. By every measure—cost, affordability, availability, job creation, and reliability—coal is by far the best energy source for base-load electricity. Due to practical, feasible advancements, the coal-fired power plants being built today emit 90 percent fewer pollutants (SO_2, NOx, particulates, and mercury) than the plants they replace from the 1970s. The bottom line: American coal is plentiful, relatively inexpensive, and ours—and we ought to make the most of new clean-coal technology.

Third, we should enhance and develop the proven technologies of coal-to-liquid fuels and coal synfuels. Liquefied coal or coal synfuels have been utilized for seventy years elsewhere in the world. Every jet departing Johannesburg, South Africa, is powered by coal synfuel. And, pursuant to a law we passed during my days in the U.S. Senate, the U.S. Air Force successfully flight-tested coal-based jet fuel in bombers and fighter jets. In March 2008, a B-1 Bomber flew faster than the speed of sound on coal synfuel, and in August of 2008 an F-15 flew at Mach 2 with a 50-50 coal synfuel jet fuel mixture. Coal synfuel is a "drop-in" fuel that does not require engine modifications, and it is cleaner than the oil we import from Venezuela and Saudi Arabia. To their credit, governors Mitch Daniels of Indiana, Brian Schweitzer of Montana, John Hoeven of North Dakota, and Haley Barbour of Mississippi have been working to encourage the development of these new clean coal-to-gas and coal-to-liquid technologies in their states. Their good example should be followed by others.

Fourth, the federal government needs to back off and let the States explore the energy resources off their coasts. According to conservative estimates from the Minerals Management Service (MMS), the taxpayer-owned lands off our coasts contain a mean estimate of 420 trillion cubic feet of natural gas. That's enough natural gas to heat all residential homes in the United States for ninety-three years. In Virginia, we've been trying for six years to escape the federal moratorium (now officially expired but still de facto in effect until the Federal government approves leases to the states) on exploring and developing offshore energy. We don't understand why, if we want to, we can't explore for energy fifty miles off our own coasts while the Castro brothers, Russia, and the People's Republic of China are drilling for oil and natural gas just fifty miles off the coast of Florida.

Here is a prime example of how cockeyed and convoluted our national energy policy is: The administration in Washington announced in late 2009 that American taxpayers have made a guaranteed mammoth loan to Brazil's state-owned oil company to extract oil and gas off Brazil's coast. Meanwhile, the same federal government prevents Virginia from allowing private American oil companies to explore off our coast and grant Virginia royalties on any development. If we in Virginia were allowed to explore our coast for oil and gas benefiting our state and our country, other coastal states would surely do the same, bringing more money into state treasuries and, more important, increasing the supply and lowering the price of energy for the United States.

We also need to explore for oil and natural gas on the barren North Slope of Alaska. The energy-savvy people of Alaska strongly support the safe exploration for oil in a small (but energy-rich) part of the Arctic National Wildlife Refuge (ANWR). That oil could be tied into the nearby Trans-Alaska Pipeline from Prudhoe Bay. Critics from outside Alaska say this exploration would hurt the environment and portray the area as if it were Yellowstone Park. I have been there with my father in summer and winter. I've seen with my own eyes that the North Slope of Alaska is a flat, treeless plain. In the summer, it is filled with enormous mosquitoes. In the winter, it is like the dark side of the moon, frozen, with virtually no light.

According to the U.S. Department of Energy, ANWR could produce 1.37 million barrels of oil a day, roughly equivalent to our
daily imports from Saudi Arabia (1.52 million barrels). Wouldn't we
prefer to buy American oil, creating American jobs, and keeping
our money here, rather than buy—and be dependent on—oil from
overseas?

Fifth, the regulatory barriers to building the next generation of
nuclear power plants need to be removed. Beyond the enormous
costs and time for building a nuclear reactor is the question of dis-
posal of the highly reactive waste. The federal government has
punted for years on the promised need for a national repository for
spent fuel, and done nothing to promote or allow nuclear fuel
reprocessing, recycling, pebble-bed reactors, and other safe pro-
duction methods of nuclear power. The French recycle and
reprocess their nuclear waste, and vitrify or encase their spent fuel
in glass, which is a safer and more efficient manner. Absurdly, the
only reason the United States is not reprocessing nuclear fuel is
because of prohibitions imposed by President Jimmy Carter in the
late 1970s. We must repeal these ineffective, burdensome restrictions. We know that if the French can do it, so can Americans!

BLOCK THAT KICK

Just as we need to pursue the five goals outlined above, America
needs to play tenacious defense to block five harmful, costly, and
counterproductive burdens that threaten our American way of life.

First, we need to block any new carbon and energy taxes. These
proposals include cap and trade energy tax schemes that would
impose higher electricity, clothes, food, and fuel costs on
American families. Middle and lower-middle income families
would be most harmed by these regressive, higher energy costs.

Second, we need to defend jobs and investments against expensive, job-killing climate regulations. German Chancellor Angela Merkel recently stated that she would not allow EU climate regulations that "would endanger jobs or investments in Germany." Our government must follow suit and vow to defend American jobs, wealth, and sovereignty from costly UN climate regulations.

Third, we need to halt the Environmental Protection Agency's attempts to regulate carbon dioxide through the Clean Air Act. The Clean Air Act was designed to regulate regional air pollutants, not global concentrations of carbon dioxide. Our government needs to apply a cost-benefit analysis to the Environmental Protection Agency's expensive, draconian proposal that will destroy American jobs and put us at a competitive disadvantage with countries like China, India, Brazil, and Russia, who will not impose such regulatory costs on their citizens or economies.

Carbon dioxide is a colorless, odorless gas that forms the basis of all plant, animal, and human life on earth. The truth is 96 percent of all CO_2 in our atmosphere occurs naturally from oceans, trees, and land; and it is increasingly apparent that the remaining 4 percent due to human activity has a negligible effect on global temperatures.

Fourth, we need to block attacks on America's largest source of energy: coal.

Coal generates about 50 percent of our electricity (20 percent comes from natural gas, another 20 percent comes from nuclear power, 7 percent comes from hydroelectric power, and only 3 percent comes from solar, wind, geothermal, waste, and other forms of "alternative" energy combined). Unlike intermittent, highly subsidized wind and solar power, American coal is reliable, affordable, and proven. We need to make the most of it.

Fifth, we need to deflect unrealistic biofuel mandates that drive up the cost of our food and feed. Using food and feed for fuel is like busting up furniture to put in a woodstove for heat. (And then folks would wonder why we're sitting on the floor.)

DEFEND, FEED, AND FUEL

A free, sovereign, and prosperous nation must be able to defend, feed, and fuel itself. When international politicians and government officials meet at United Nations-sponsored climate change conferences in Copenhagen, Cancun, or elsewhere, they contrive new ways to transfer America's wealth and inveigle us into unilateral economic disarmament. They want to impose regulations that put us at a competitive disadvantage in the global marketplace.

Energy propels our American economy. At a time when families and businesses are struggling to make ends meet, we should not put America's economy on a scheme of ever-tightening energy rationing. Instead, we should be developing affordable, reliable American energy resources.

We must stop punting the ball year after year to sanctimonious social engineers who hobble America with job-killing policies.

We want to keep the ball and score with practical conservation. American clean coal technologies, American nuclear power, natural gas and oil, batteries, solar, waste-to-energy—we have a diversity of supply in our playbook. When it comes to energy, there is no single silver bullet—we need silver buckshot! It's time for Washington to encourage energy rearmament in the United States.

America deserves an innovative, winning energy game plan, unleashing American creativity and resources for American jobs, competitiveness, national security, and American energy freedom.

CHAPTER SEVEN

THERE'S NO PLACE LIKE HOME

IF YOU WANT TO BE A BASEBALL STAR FOR THE MINNESOTA Twins, it helps to have a unique name—and a game well suited to the Twins' unconventional ballpark. Or so it would seem from the strange-but-glorious history of the Major League Baseball franchise that moved away from Washington, D.C.

Minnesota's tradition of fielding star players with unusual names began in the '60s and early '70s when Harmon Killebrew, Camilo Pascual, Jim Kaat, and Zoilo Versalles starred for Minnesota. It continued through the late '70s and '80s when Bert Blyleven, Kent Hrbek, Gary Gaetti, and Tom Brunansky led Minnesota to an unlikely world championship. And it kicked into overdrive during the '90s and '00s when Chuck Knoblauch, Doug Mientkiewicz, Torii Hunter, and A. J. Pierzynski all broke into the big leagues wearing a Minnesota uniform.

Not surprisingly, these unusual names sometimes captured the creative imagination of opposing teams' fans. One clever home-made banner from the '80s incorporated a saying from Pat Sajak's *Wheel of Fortune* TV game show while poking fun at Minnesota's star first baseman. It read: *Hey, Hrbek, Buy a Vowel!*

While the Twins player names were often unconventional, the ballpark where they played for many years was even more unusual.

Known as the Hubert H. Humphrey Metrodome, the inflatable-roof stadium was home to the Twins and the NFL's Minnesota Vikings during the '80s, '90s, and '00s. This shared arrangement meant that some football seats had to be temporarily removed and stacked out of the way during baseball games. And it meant that rather than having a solid outfield fence beyond right (and right-center) field, the Metrodome instead featured a long sheet of removable black plastic stretched in front of the stacked seats. This "Hefty bag" fence was unlike the fencing in any other Major League ballpark. And it, along with several other unusual features—a very bouncy artificial turf, a white interior roof that some-times hid fly balls, and the reverberating sounds of Minnesota's vocal indoor crowd—combined to make the Metrodome an espe-cially tough place for opposing teams to play.

In 1987, for example, the Twins won fifty-six of their eighty-one home games, but only twenty-nine of their eighty-one away games. Despite their abysmal road record, the Twins' success at home carried them to an improbable division championship in the mediocre American League West. (Had the Twins been com-peting in the American League East, their 85–77 record would have earned them only a fourth-place finish.)

Unsurprisingly, the Twins entered the post-season playoffs as heavy underdogs. Nonetheless, Minnesota caught a break because the playoff schedule that year gave them home field advantage in both the American League Championship Series and the World Series. (Back then, MLB did not award home field advantage in the post-season to the team with the better overall record; they simply rotated this advantage from year to year between divisions and between leagues.)

So, the Twins entered the playoffs knowing that if they could win at home, they could become World Champions without ever having to win a game on the road. And to help them in their quest, the *Minneapolis Star-Tribune* advocated one of the most popular promotional gimmicks ever to come along in sports. I'm referring, of course, to the "Homer Hanky."

"MY BABY WAVES THE HOMER HANKY"

A simple white handkerchief with the red Twins insignia screenprinted on it, the Homer Hanky was distributed for free to all 53,000 fans attending the first game of the playoffs in the Metrodome. To further hype this fun promotion, a number of aerobic dance teams performed in a "Homer Hanky Dance-Off" prior to the game. And once the game began, the Twins' public address announcer periodically played a raucous re-make of the 1966 hit, "(My Baby Does the) Hanky Panky"—only this time, the words were changed to, "My Baby Waves the Homer Hanky."

The effect was exhilarating. The Minnesota home crowd spent much of the game waving their hankies and yelling as loud as humanly possible. As Kent Hrbek described it: "The place was electric. It was just rocking.... The fans were going to try to help us and screaming their lungs out was the way they were going to do it. It actually felt electric. There was something in the air. Not only could you hear it, but you could actually feel how excited people were."

Buoyed by this fan support, the Twins won that first playoff game. And they never looked back. They beat the Detroit Tigers in five games to take the American League pennant, and then beat the downriver St. Louis Cardinals in seven games to win the World Series. Over the course of the two series, Minnesota won every single post-season game they played at home, thanks in no small part to the "Dome Magic" that the team felt when playing inside that unique, loud Minneapolis Metrodome.

"Man, the noise of the crowd, it was the loudest place in baseball," asserted Twins pitcher Frank Viola. And this claim was no exaggeration. In fact, the Minnesota Pollution Control Agency placed noise monitors inside the stadium during the playoffs—and the decibel readings frequently exceeded those for jet plane takeoffs!

This crowd noise helped give the Twins a feeling of invincibility at home. As Viola sensed, "Once you start feeling good about where you're playing and you get the support that we got, we never expected to lose there."

"DÉJÀ VU ALL OVER AGAIN"

As improbable as that 1987 World Championship was, Minnesota turned around and did it again four years later in 1991. And they did it in an eerily similar fashion, winning every playoff game at home—while losing every World Series game on the road.

Just as the 1987 Twins had the honor of being the World Champions with the worst regular season record in Major League Baseball history (up to that point), the 1991 Twins enjoyed an equally dubious distinction. They were the first team in Major League Baseball history to win the World Series after finishing last in their division the previous year. Interestingly, Minnesota earned this distinction by beating an Atlanta Braves team in the World Series that had also finished last in their division the year before.

That 1991 World Series was a classic. Baseball Commissioner Fay Vincent called it "probably the greatest World Series ever," and it's easy to see why. Five of the games were decided by a single run. Four ended with the winning run being scored in the home team's final at-bat. Three of the games—including the last two in Minnesota—went into extra innings.

And one unmistakable truth was proved yet again by the Minnesota Twins' success: There's no place like home.

That's right, there's nothing like having a home field advantage—playing in a familiar place where you know the ballpark's peculiarities and have enthusiastic fans rooting for your success.

Regrettably, this truth is one that many policymakers in Washington fail to appreciate—or respect. Rather than deferring to the wisdom of the people and their state governments, rather than keeping the federal government to its few "enumerated powers" outlined in the U.S. Constitution, many elites in Washington act as "lords," thinking they know better than their "subjects." They look for centralized, nationally imposed prescriptions for local concerns, preferring top-down, one-size-fits-all policies handed down by disconnected Washington "professionals" rather than leaving these matters to state and local governments or private citizens in their communities. These Washington elites are usurping the prerogatives of "We the People," even though common sense is not very common in Washington. That's why many of us who don't live in the Lone Star State appreciate and admire their slogan

"Don't Mess with Texas!" Fundamentally, the elites are opposed to letting you and me and our local elected officials develop our own ideas and solutions in ways that draw on the unique character, history, people, and resources of our communities. In the process, what the lords in Washington are really doing is denying us our liberty to govern ourselves.

THE GAME PLAN

In sports, every team develops a "customized" game plan based on extensive "inside" knowledge of the strengths of its own players, the playing field, and a careful analysis of the opposing team. The game plan is a strategy for success, and the best game plans are both very particular and flexible to take advantage of changing circumstances. What makes for a good game plan also makes for good government. It needs to be particular, it needs to be flexible, and it should acknowledge the character—the particular strengths, weaknesses, and circumstances—of the team. The people of Las Vegas have different values and needs—and ways of achieving them—than, say, relatively nearby Salt Lake City. Oklahoma City needs a different "game plan" than does San Diego. The people of Columbus, Georgia, might very well have different priorities than the people of Columbus, Ohio.

The founders understood this diversity well, though the United States was far less diverse and far smaller than it is today. When the several States created the United States, they did not desire to establish a strong central government that imposed uniformity on their many varied aspects of life. Instead, they established a "federalist" system of government built on the foundational idea that the government closest to the people—and most responsive to the people's wishes and aspirations—should have the greatest latitude over most public matters. Indeed, the United States Constitution lays out an important though modest role for the federal government—mostly limited to external relations and providing a national defense, maintaining a common currency, protecting individual rights, and preserving unfettered inter-state commerce. The federal government was never intended to interfere in every state and local concern—in fact, the Constitution was designed to prevent that from happening. The states were meant to govern themselves, and they still do, though an intrusive federal government looms ever larger and more threateningly over them.

Today, for example, states are still allowed to choose for themselves whether they want to be a "closed-shop union state" where joining a union can be a condition of employment, or a "right to work state" where joining a union is not compulsory. Personally, I strongly support right-to-work laws as a matter of personal liberty, but other people in other parts of the country see this issue differently and have passed laws in their states upholding a requirement of union membership as a condition of employment in certain fields.

When I was governor of Virginia, we used these differences in state law to our competitive advantage, establishing a "game plan" to attract jobs to our state that emphasized our "home field advantage" as the northern-most right-to-work state along the eastern seaboard. We found that most companies eliminated any state from consideration that did not have a Right-to-Work law. During my four years in office, we recruited companies from elsewhere in the United States, as well as Canada, Europe, Asia, and Australia, to Virginia. A number of major corporations—including Siemens, Motorola, IBM, Toshiba, Volvo Truck, Oracle, GE Fanuc, Georgia Pacific, Whitehall Robins, Reynolds Metals, Fleetwood, Parkdale, Holtzbrinck Publishing, Carter-Wallace, New Millennium, Boise

Cascade, Hershey, Diebold, Gilbert Lumber, Gateway, B.I. Chemicals, TXi Chapparal Steel, Frito-Lay, Target, Best Buy, Dollar Tree, Family Dollar, Dollar General, Kohl's, Coors, R.R. Donnelley, Maple Leaf Bakery, Nippon Wiper Blades, Canon, Oji-Yuka Yupo, VFP, Ferguson, RGC Minerals, Industrial Galvinizers, Vaughan, Capital One, Sumitomo, Toray, Genworth, Pittston, Barr Labs, ATCC, Geico, Chubb, Hewlett-Packard, BGF Porcher, Maersk, K-Line, Ericsson, Iceland Seafood, Dynax, Strongwell, Avis, Drake Extrusion, Haller Clocks, Lillian Vernon, Goodyear, Yokohama Tire, ASB Greenworld, Foot Levelers, Royal, B.A. Mullican, T.D. Wheel, Kraft Foods, Hood, Abbott Laboratories, Diversity Food Processing, Scholle, Woodstook Manufacturing, Meadville Forging, Westvaco, Electro-Mechanical, Groendyk, Abell Industries, A.O. Smith, Jouan, and many others—built, relocated, or expanded major manufacturing, service, and/or distribution centers in Virginia. Companies chose Virginia for their new investment because, among other reasons, we had competitively lower taxes, lower energy costs, a highly skilled work force, a strategic location, and right-to-work laws that were seen as helping keep labor-management relations harmonious. (One effect of right-to-work laws is that they encourage unions to be more responsive to their members, because no one can be compelled to join.)

LABORATORIES OF DEMOCRACY

In a federalist system, each state can capitalize on, or seek to create, its own advantages. For example, some states—like Florida, Texas, Tennessee, Nevada, and New Hampshire—have eschewed a state income tax as a way of attracting investment and jobs. In crafting policies and laws that reflect the needs of the people they serve, the States serve as "laboratories of democracy," where diverse policy ideas can be tried and tested. Similar to scientists who make new discoveries or coaches who develop innovative new schemes for their players, government reformers who find new and better ways to carry out the people's wishes will often find others eager to imitate their success.

The migration of people to communities and states is proof of ideas and policies that attract investment, jobs, and opportunities for prosperity. Forty-nine of the top fifty growing areas are the West and South. Population growth and movement to Mountain West and Southern states in the past several decades is an indication that more people see a better opportunity to achieve their dreams in places with a better quality of life due to lower taxes, fewer regulations, and thus more opportunity than what generally exists in areas that are losing population.

I've met and worked with many inspirational governors, like Bobby Jindal of Louisiana who has been a leader in needed ethics reform in his state, Haley Barbour of Mississippi who demonstrated tremendous leadership in the wake of Hurricane Katrina and has attracted unprecedented international investment to his state, and such Hall of Fame governors as Carroll Campbell (South Carolina), John Engler (Michigan), Frank Keating (Oklahoma), George Pataki (New York), Bill Weld (Massachusetts), Tommy Thompson (Wisconsin), Ed Schafer and John Hoeven (North Dakota), Terry Branstad (Iowa), Jeb Bush and Lawton Chiles (Florida), John Y. Brown (Kentucky), Jim Hunt (North Carolina), William Donald Schaeffer (Maryland), Bill Owens and Roy Roemer (Colorado), Ed Rendell and Tom Ridge (Pennsylvania), Mitch Daniels (Indiana), Tom Carper (Delaware), Christine Todd Whitman (New Jersey), Zell Miller and Sonny Perdue (Georgia), George Voinovich (Ohio), Mike Huckabee (Arkansas), and Howard Dean (Vermont). And that's not to mention Ronald Reagan, Bill

Clinton, and George W. Bush—three governors who became presidents. These governors were all successful reformers, though their philosophies of government were different. They pursued different strategies geared to the different needs of their communities, the times in which they served, and the policy prescriptions they had offered that won them strong support of the people of their state. It would have been a tragedy to strait jacket these governors with restrictive federal mandates set by far-away bureaucrats—but that is what Washington does on an ever-increasing basis. It needs to stop.

During my time as governor of Virginia—with a Democratic majority in our legislature and reduction of 10,000 state employees—we made a number of successful policy innovations that were eventually emulated in other states. One was bringing academic accountability to schools through objective testing that could chart student progress. Our Champion Schools Initiative and School Performance Report Cards were developed by and for the people of Virginia. We made these educational improvements on our own, without being told to do so by a swarm of bureaucrats in Washington or because it was mandated by Goals 2000, the No-Child-Left-Behind Act, or any other federal program.

As rigorous academic accountability has taken root in our schools, schoolchildren have acquired the educational proficiency and knowledge to compete and succeed in the international marketplace. And in the many years since we passed our Standards of Learning, nothing has made me prouder than the continued accolades Virginia has received as our students and public schools are consistently rated among the very best in the United States— which is why other states have tried to copy our reforms.

Similarly, while I was governor, we were one of the first states to comprehensively reform our welfare laws, implementing statewide the most pro-work and pro-family reforms in the United

States (and we needed a waiver from the Clinton Administration to implement our law). Leading the reforms, and doing so superbly, was my Secretary of Health and Human Resources Kay Coles James, who herself had been on welfare as a child. Among the reforms: We established paternity in cases involving out-of-wedlock births (to better ensure that fathers were at least financially responsible for the support of their children). We required unwed teen mothers to stay at home and in school. And we set a two-year limit on how long one could receive aid (reminding people that welfare assistance is to be a temporary condition, not a permanent way of life). The requirement that mothers identify the father of their child as a condition of receiving any aid refreshed many recollections, and Virginia has the highest paternity identification rate (99 percent) in the United States. Welfare rolls are now much lower, and taxpayers have saved hundreds of millions of dollars a year. Best of all, tens of thousands of Virginians and their families have moved from lives of dependency to self-sufficiency and the dignity of holding a job.

In time, reforms like ours and those championed by then Governor Tommy Thompson of Wisconsin were adopted by other states—and by the weaker federal welfare reform law passed in late 1996. We measured welfare reform success not by how many people were receiving government checks, but rather by how many people were living independent, self-reliant lives within a family.

Another successful policy "experiment" from my time as governor focused on reducing violent crime. In our state prior to my term as governor, three-fourths of all crimes were being committed by repeat offenders, and violent crime rates were skyrocketing. Virginians agreed with our decisive proposal to abolish Virginia's lenient, liberal, dishonest parole system that was releasing violent criminals after serving only one-fourth of their sentence.

At the press conference where I announced our plan to fix the parole system, I introduced two courageous women. They had been raped by the same man, the second woman after the rapist had been released early on parole. My pledge was that our reform would prevent tragedies like this through the keystone of our reform agenda: Truth-in-Sentencing, which would ensure that when a judge or jury sentences a convicted rapist to twelve years, he serves twelve years, not three. For those felons incarcerated for crimes committed before the abolition of parole, I appointed a parole board comprised of crime victims and frontline law enforcement professionals. Parole, which had been granted more than 40 percent of the time in pervious years, fell to single digits under the experienced judgment of our new board members. Our criminal justice reforms led not only to substantial increases in the time served by violent felons, especially repeat offenders, but in double digit reduction in violent crime and juvenile crime.

Who was helped the most by these historic reforms that in just a few years reduced violent crime by 16 percent and juvenile crime by 13 percent? The most vulnerable among us: the elderly, women, and people in low-income housing projects and in communities stalked by fear—people who will never be a victim or a statistic because they were assaulted, raped, or even murdered by a violent criminal who was released early on parole.

Another factor contributing to the protection of law-abiding citizens was the passage of a "concealed-carry" gun law in Virginia during my time as governor. This measure, whose General Assembly patron was then-state Senator Virgil Goode, was vigorously opposed by some gun control advocates in our state. They feared Virginia would begin to resemble the shootout at the OK Corral. But we were able to allay some of their concerns by pointing to the successful track record of Florida—a fellow "laboratory for democracy" that had previously implemented a concealed carry law. Since adopting this law in 1995, Virginia has not become like Tombstone in 1881. In fact, Virginia remains a much safer place to live, work, raise a family, and visit than our liberal neighbors to the north, the District of Columbia and Maryland.

Of course, there is still more to do to combat the scourge of drugs and gang violence that endanger our young people. But in Virginia we have shown that common-sense policies can improve the safety of law-abiding citizens. The evidence is clear that Truth-in-Sentencing is much more effective in reducing the crime rate than taking away the Second Amendment rights of law-abiding citizens.

The bigger point is that it is desirable for diverse state governments to experiment with public policy solutions. So long as they are not infringing on our rights or interfering with interstate commerce, the people in the individual states should have the right to chart their own destiny with policies consistent with their own values. This sovereignty also protects the freedom of the people in the states to learn from each other and assess certain beneficial policy approaches compared to others on their own playing field.

LEARNING FROM EXPERIENCE

One of the most important lessons that sports teaches is this: it pays to learn from your own mistakes—and from the mistakes of others. One great illustration of this is a famous "home field advantage" incident.

In 1934, the Chicago Bears and New York Giants faced off in the NFL Championship game on a frozen field at New York's Polo Grounds. The Bears, led by owner and coach George Halas, came into the game as heavy favorites. Not only were they the defending

NFL champions, they were undefeated in the 1934 regular season and had a stifling defense.

The Giants, meanwhile, had stumbled to an 8–5 record. They had lost twice to Chicago in the regular season (by a combined score of 37–16) and had scored barely half as many points (147) as the Bears had (286) during the season.

The night before the game, New York experienced a freezing rain, making the Polo Grounds' frozen field especially slippery on game day, with temperatures reportedly as low as nine degrees. Not surprisingly, both teams struggled to find their footing early in the game. After seeing his players slip and slide all over the field with ineffective cleats, New York coach Steve Owen dispatched his equipment manager, Abe Cohen, to find shoes with better traction—specifically, "gym sneakers." Since it was Sunday, the New York department stores were closed. So Cohen went to the Manhattan College athletic department, borrowed eight pairs of sneakers, and took them back to the Polo Grounds in time for the second half of the game. The Bears were leading 10–3 at the half.

Wearing these borrowed sneakers, the Giants staged a remarkable second-half comeback, outmaneuvering the slipping and sliding Bears and scoring 27 points in the fourth quarter to win the game, 30–13.

Most accounts of this memorable game end here, with the Giants' unusual exploitation of their "home field advantage"— being able to borrow sneakers from their Manhattan College neighbors. But there's more to the story.

Twenty-nine years later, I was on the sidelines up against ice cold brick walls at Wrigley Field in Chicago when these same two franchises squared off again in the famous frozen 1963 NFL Championship Game. George "Papa Bear" Halas was still coaching the Chicago Bears. The old coach undoubtedly remembered the advantage the borrowed sneakers had given the New York Giants on a frozen field three decades earlier.

So, as his team prepared to play on a hard-frozen surface at Chicago's Wrigley Field, Coach Halas had Bears quarterback Bill Wade wear a pair of high top sneakers in the biggest game of his life. And, set up by two interception returns by the vaunted Bears' defense, Wade ran two quarterback "sneaks" for touchdowns that day to secure Chicago's 14–10 victory over the prolific Y. A. Tittle-led Giants offense.

I was thrilled at Bill Wade's success, because he was one of the nicest players I've ever known. Indeed, Wade taught me quarterback drills. Reinforcing one of my father's rules for his children, Wade never swore ("dadgummit" was the closest he'd come to cussing), and he'd always sign his autograph with a cross "+."

But Wade's performance that day is etched in my memory for another reason—because it stands as a great example of the importance that sports gives to learning from the past. George Halas remembered that game from twenty-nine years earlier, and he made sure that sneakers would be available for his quarterback that frigid championship game day. As Paul Harvey liked to say, "Now you know the rest of the story."

Similarly, public policymakers need to learn from their own trial-and-error experiences—and those of others. They need to learn how to utilize their "home field advantage" for the benefit of their citizens.

The way to do that is not by manipulating the national government to send a disproportionate amount of federal "pork" to one's state or Congressional district, but by promoting a renewed appreciation for the founders' federalist vision. The founders did not want the federal government interfering in the internal affairs of states and localities. They overthrew the distant, arrogant British monarchy on the Thames, and we must not countenance a new American House of Lords on the Potomac ruling our states as if the Tenth Amendment of the Bill of Rights was never ratified.

If government needs to be involved in an issue, the government closest to the people is always better than bringing in swarming, suffocating meddlers from Washington. State government has the "home field advantage" of knowing the uniqueness, values, and needs of the people in their communities to whom they are directly accountable. We live in a great, vast, and diverse country, but for each of us there's one part of it that's ours. And as the fans in Homer Hanky Minnesota, Who Dat New Orleans, and Mile High Denver already know: there's no place like home.

CHAPTER EIGHT

WHEN UMPIRES CAN'T BE TRUSTED, EVERYONE LOSES

HERE'S A TRIVIA QUESTION SURE TO BE APPRECIATED BY those who love sports and politics: What former Rhodes Scholar starred on his college basketball team, enjoyed a solid NBA career, won a silver medal in the Olympics, and served for three terms as a federal legislator where he towered over most of his Capitol Hill colleagues?

If you guessed, "Bill Bradley" you'd be close; he too was a Rhodes scholar, an NBA star, and a federal legislator. But the correct answer is Tom McMillan. Bradley won an Olympic gold medal in 1964, whereas McMillan "received" a silver in 1972.

"Received," because McMillan and his teammates on the 1972 U.S. Olympic basketball team never actually got the silver medals that were awarded them. In fact, they refused to accept them, because they did not want to confer legitimacy upon one of the most suspicious officiating decisions in Olympic sports history.

COLD WAR BASKETBALL

In the 1972 Olympics, the U.S. men's basketball team looked to extend America's domination of the sport invented by American John Naismith. Entering the Olympic Games in Munich, the United States had won seven straight gold medals and had never lost a game in international competition. After breezing through their first eight games of the 1972 Olympics, Team USA faced a tough Soviet Union team in the gold medal game.

With the score tied 49–49 and only three seconds left in the game, Doug Collins went to shoot the second of two free throws after a Soviet foul near midcourt. As Collins lifted the ball to begin his shooting motion, the horn from the scorer's table sounded, but no official stopped the game. Undeterred, Collins sank the free throw to put the U.S. ahead, 50–49.

The Soviets then inbounded the ball and began dribbling up the court. As they neared mid-court, an official stopped play with one second on the clock because of some commotion at the scorer's table. There, a Soviet coach was protesting, claiming that the USSR had called a timeout prior to Collins's second foul shot.

Whether or not the Soviets had actually called this timeout remains a matter of dispute—as does the question of whether the Soviet coach should have been assessed a technical foul for leaving the coach's area while play was underway. But the referees agreed to reset the clock and let the Soviets have a "do-over" after

Secretary General R. William Jones of the Fédération Internationale de Basketball (FIBA) came down to the court and insisted that the game's final three seconds be replayed. (Later, this official would acknowledge that he had no authority to make a ruling on a game still in progress.)

After using their timeout to set up a final play, the Soviets inbounded the ball with a full-court pass that missed its target and ended up being tipped off the backboard. The errant pass set off a wild celebration among the Americans, who had heard the horn blow while the ball was in flight and had concluded that the game was now over.

But the horn blow was actually an attempt by the officials at the scorer's table to halt play because they had not yet finished resetting the clock to three seconds. So, the referees conferred again with FIBA Secretary General Jones. And the officials decided that the Soviets would be given a third opportunity to inbound the ball and play out the game's finale.

At this point, the U.S. coaches considered pulling their team from the floor and refusing to play out the final seconds a third time. But head coach Hank Iba was concerned that departing could leave the Americans vulnerable to a Soviet appeal that the Americans had forfeited the game by exiting the court with time still on the reset clock.

So, the U.S. team remained on the court and sent their long-armed 6'11" center, future Congressman Tom McMillan, to defend the inbound passer and make it difficult for the Soviets to get the ball in play. As the official went to give the ball to the Soviet inbounder, he motioned for McMillan to back away from his opponent. Even though there was no rule in international play requiring a defender to give extra room to the passer, McMillan complied, fearing a technical foul if he refused.

With McMillan no longer obstructing his ability to inbound the ball, the Soviet inbounder threw a full-court pass to one of his teammates. Two American defenders converged on the throw, but were unable to intercept it. Both fell awkwardly to the floor as the Soviet Union's Alexandr Belov caught the ball and made a game-winning lay-up.

The U.S. team immediately filed a formal protest. But the five-man Olympic jury divided along Cold War lines (Cuba, Hungary, and Poland sided with the Soviets; Italy and Puerto Rico with the Americans). So, the Soviets were awarded the gold medal.

FROM VERY SHADY TO THOROUGHLY CORRUPT

As followers of the Olympics know, that 1972 basketball incident is hardly the only case of suspicious behavior by officials at the frequently politicized Olympic Games. For example, American boxer Roy Jones Jr. lost a bout to South Korea's Park Si-Hun at the 1988 Seoul Olympics despite landing eighty-six punches to Park's thirty-two. Reportedly, the honorable Korean boxer was so embarrassed by the "home cooking" he received from the judges that he apologized to Jones afterward. Moreover, one of the judges admitted soon after the fight that the bout's 3–2 split decision was an egregious error. And all three judges voting for Park were eventually suspended. Nonetheless, the official investigation by the International Olympic Committee found no deliberate wrongdoing by the judges, so the IOC stands by the judges' decision to this day.

At the 2002 Winter Olympics, the judging in the ice skating competition wasn't just shady—it was thoroughly corrupt. In the pairs competition, a Russian duo won the gold medal over a Canadian couple, even though the Russians had made an obvious techical mistake and the Canadians had not.

Suspicious of the ruling, Sally Stapleford of the International Skating Union's Technical Committee confronted French judge Marie-Reine Le Gougne as soon as Le Gougne returned to the officials' hotel at the end of the evening's events. Le Gougne broke down and confessed that she had been instructed by the head of the French skating organization, Didier Gailhaguet, to score the Russian pair the highest regardless of how the other skaters performed. Apparently, a secret Franco-Russian pact had been made to fix the scores of each others' top skaters so that the Russians would win gold in the ice skating pairs competition and the French would win gold in the ice dancing competition.

Le Gougne repeated her confession at a judges' meeting the next day, but later recanted and said she truly believed the Russian pair deserved to win the competition. In the end, the IOC decided to upgrade the Canadian couple's silver medals to gold, while allowing the Russian skaters to keep their golds as well (since there was no indication that these skaters were aware of the score-fixing scheme). Understandably, the French judge and the head of the French skating organization were suspended for "misconduct" and banned from judging at future Winter Olympics.

While nationalistic pride has been the fuel behind farcical, biased scoring by East German diving judges and most other officiating scandals in the Olympic Games, greed served as the motivation for the recent refereeing controversy that rocked the National Basketball Association. In 2007, NBA referee Tim Donaghy pled guilty in U.S. District Court to allegations that he had participated in a gambling conspiracy to fix the outcome and point spread of numerous NBA games that he had officiated. NBA commissioner David Stern characterized Donaghy as a "rogue official," and no charges were ever brought against any other NBA referees, even though Donaghy claimed that others had, on occasion, fixed the outcome of games. Still, like other sports gambling scandals—such as Pete Rose betting on baseball games he managed and the Chicago "Black Sox" conspiring to lose the 1919 World Series in exchange for gambling proceeds—the Donaghy scandal cast a shadow over the fundamental integrity of these athletic competitions.

WHEN WRIGHT WAS WRONG

During a Monday Night Football broadcast, ESPN's announcer Mike Tirico articulated why so many people love to watch the live drama of sporting events. "This is why sports is so cool," Tirico observed. "You don't know what script is going to play out."

Few characteristics are more important to spectator sports—and to government—than integrity and legitimacy. In a competitive, dog-eat-dog world, no one likes to lose or to see his team lose, although one can accept a loss and strive to fight another day if one believes it was a fair fight or contest.

When, however, people have reason to question the impartiality of those presiding over the proceedings, it is very difficult for a sports league—or a representative government—to engender respect. When the umpires can't be trusted, everyone loses. It puts in doubt the legitimacy of every outcome; it makes a mockery of fairness.

Thankfully, in the world of sports, corruption among officials is rare. And the use of new technology to correct mistakes by officials in football, hockey, tennis, horse racing, and other sports has sought to improve the accuracy of "close calls." Indeed, writer Daniel Henninger believes sports is one of the last places in American society where clearly defined rules are widely accepted and respected.

Henninger penned a column for the *Wall Street Journal* entitled, "If Sports Ruled the World." In it, he recounted the melodramatic—

and anti-climatic—conclusion to the 2009 U.S. Open women's tennis semi-finals. Here's what happened: Defending champion Serena Williams was serving to Kim Clijsters, a lower-ranked opponent who had played so well all day that she only needed two more points to complete a stunning upset. At this critical juncture in the match, the line judge called Williams for a foot fault on her second serve, giving Clijsters a point, and bringing the contest to "match point."

Before serving again, Williams protested the call in a rude manner (for tennis), dropping a couple of "f bombs" as she threatened to physically harm the official. Williams' tirade constituted what tennis calls a "code violation" (the equivalent of an unsportsmanlike conduct penalty in football). This meant that the head official had to penalize Williams one additional point—making Clijsters the winner. Game. Set. Match.

In writing about the head official's willingness to enforce the rules against a star player at a crucial time in the match, Henninger said: "This is why we watch sports. Not just to see the thrill of victory and the agony of defeat, but because it is the one world left with clear rules abided by all. Compared to sports, real life has become constant chaos."

Henninger mentions several examples of how, in our political life, rules appear to be flouted, including an instance where then House Speaker Jim Wright "got around a rule that a defeated vote couldn't be redone for 24 hours. Mr. Wright adjourned the House, brought it back to order in minutes, and called it a 'new' legislative day. The House clerk even said that Oct. 29 had suddenly become Oct. 30.…"

More recently, he notes, the Obama administration's "[Attorney General]" Eric Holder's decision to let a prosecutor investigate CIA interrogations that were ruled inbounds years ago is like a baseball commissioner reversing a hotly disputed World Series home run. Fans everywhere would burn down the stadium."

And he notes that while in Washington there is a battle between those who believe that the Constitution should be interpreted as the founders intended (the Justice Scalia, "originalist," or "strict constructionist" view) and those who believe it should be interpreted as liberal empathy would dictate (the Obama administration view), "in the primal world of sports we are all strict constructionists. . . . "

It is true that we are all "strict constructionists" when it comes to sports in that no one in sports would ever accept a rules change in the middle of the game. No one in sports would ever accept the kind of rules-flaunting shenanigans that Jim Wright pulled that day in the House of Representatives—even though situations arise periodically in sports that cry out for some sort of remedy.

One prime example comes from the grand old days of the National Football League. Until the late 1970s, NFL goal posts were actually placed on the goal line, not the back line of the end zone. As my friend Tony Mercurio of ESPN Radio in Tidewater, Virginia, reminds his faithful listeners, in the original "post" patterns, the receiver would use the base of the goal posts to screen the defensive back from the pass play.

SLINGIN' SAMMY'S SILLY SAFETY

Slingin' Sammy Baugh starred for the Washington Redskins back in the days when football players wore leather helmets and often played offense and defense, and on special teams. Baugh was one of nine men selected to be in the charter class of the Pro Football Hall of Fame. And it's easy to see why.

As a quarterback, Baugh won a record-setting six NFL passing titles. As a safety, he was the first player ever to intercept four passes in a single game. And as a punter, Baugh still holds the single-season NFL record for average yards per kick (50.1).

In 1943, Baugh became the only player in NFL history ever to lead the league in passing, punting, and interceptions in the same season. (Amazingly, he threw for four touchdowns—and caught four interceptions—in one memorable game that year.) And Slingin' Sammy led Washington to the NFL championship game five times, winning two.

What's more, Baugh would have won a third championship title if not for one of the most bizarre plays in NFL history.

In the 1945 NFL Championship Game, the Washington Redskins squared off against the Cleveland Rams. Early in the game, the Redskins had the ball on their own 5-yard line. Baugh dropped back to pass from his own end zone, but when he threw the ball towards an open receiver, it clanged off the goal post and fell to the ground.

According to NFL rules in 1945, any forward pass out of the end zone that hit the goal posts was ruled a safety. This peculiar rule hardly ever had to be invoked, because most teams back then did not pass much—especially out of their own end zone. (Before pass-happy pioneers like Baugh, most teams regarded the forward pass as a last-ditch act of desperation rather than an integral part of an effective offense.)

Nevertheless, rules are rules. So, even though the pass-that-hits-the-posts rule was half-baked, Cleveland rightfully received two points on that day back in 1945. And, as fate would have it, these two points proved to make all the difference in the game as Baugh's Redskins went down to defeat by a final score of 15–14.

After seeing his team lose the NFL championship game because of that peculiar rule, Redskins owner George Preston Marshall was so mad that he spent the off-season advocating for a rules change. Not wishing to see a repeat of that bizarre 1945 incident, the NFL rules committee readily adopted what came to be known as the "Baugh/Marshall Rule." It said that any forward pass striking the goal posts would, from henceforth, be ruled incomplete.

It's especially notable that, though virtually everyone involved in the 1945 championship game thought this a ridiculous way for Cleveland to score two points, no one at the time argued for a middle-of-the-game rules change. No big-shot NFL official came down out of the stands and instructed the officials to give Slingin' Sammy and the Redskins a "do-over." No "Jim-Wright-thinking" referee tried to make up a new rule on the fly to bring about a more desirable result, or "deem" it an incomplete pass. Instead, everyone acknowledged that the game should be played under the existing rules—and that any rules changes ought to be made by the NFL's legislative body, the rules committee, at an appropriate time later.

In other words, everyone at the time agreed to the "rule of law"—to the idea that we are all subject to abide by the rules as written, even if we think them undesirable or ridiculous. At times, laws will be asinine, reflecting the imperfections of the lawmakers who wrote them. But, especially as bad laws can be corrected by good ones, it is better to live under the "rule of law" than to let people ignore or abrogate contracts, laws, and established rules of engagement in a free marketplace of goods, products, and services. It is better to live under the rule of law than to let each and every individual decide in the middle of the game what rules he wants to follow—or what day in October he wants to pretend it is.

These days, many family-owned car dealerships rightfully take exception to the government taking their tax money to loan, invest, and otherwise prop up failing, faltering, government-favored auto manufacturers. When the government intervenes to protect some manufacturers, it tilts what should be a level playing field and instead favors not only certain car manufacturing companies, but the dealers affiliated with them.

Automobile dealers are valued employers and good corporate citizens in many communities—and it doesn't matter whether these dealers sell cars made by American, Japanese, Korean, Swedish, German, French, Italian, or British companies. (We should remember that even many "foreign" cars are actually manufactured here in America.) Our government should provide a level playing field of competition where consumers decide which dealership or manufacturer provides the best service or products. The government should be impartial—another word for fair—and abide by the rules of our free market system. It should not change the rules to pick favorites.

Sports fans, and all Americans, should be riled and displeased by government umpires in sky boxes changing the rules of competition in a manner that is wrong as a matter of economic principle, policy, and legislative process.

WEARING TEAM COLORS
UNDER THEIR ROBES

There are some in the judicial branch of government who don't want to be bound by the rules as written. They want to be able to "fix" the rules in the middle of the game to achieve their preferred results. They don't care if these results are inconsistent with the original intent of the Constitution or with legislation passed by elected representatives of the people.

These judicial activists want to be able to use their position of authority to "fix" societal problems—irrespective of whether this requires them to bend the rules or reinterpret our "living Constitution" to reflect their personal preferences or political views.

Unfortunately, when judges seek to "fix" societal problems by legislating from the bench, they cease to be impartial umpires fairly administering the law. They become, in effect, players dressed as referees. Their efforts to "fix" the law (rather than leaving that job where it belongs, with legislators and the voters) compromises the integrity of our entire system of government just as that rogue NBA official compromised the integrity of his sport when he "fixed" the games he was officiating. It is the job of officials, judges, and referees to enforce the rules, to apply the law. It is not their job to make up the rules or to create the law.

But we have activist judges who don't care if people in certain school districts or states would like to have the Pledge of Allegiance recited in their schools. Instead of obeying the will of the people, they banned the Pledge because of the words, "Under God."

We have seen judges—including those on the U.S. Supreme Court—allow the lords in New London, Connecticut, to take people's homes, the American dream, not for a school, a road, or some other public purpose, but because they want to derive more tax revenue from that property. We the People are not subjects of any crown or government. These are some of the affronts which were cause for our secession from the British monarchy.

That's why we need judges in the United States, especially federal judges who are appointed for life, who understand that the role of a judge is to apply the law, not invent the law or amend our Bill of Rights by judicial decree.

The fact that so many judges ignore their clear constitutional role is one reason why I believe that federal judges should not be appointed to their positions for life, but should serve long (perhaps 12-year) terms.

When judges cease to be impartial umpires and instead become "law-fixers," they sometimes wreak far more havoc on our society than would ever be wreaked by a legislative body directly accountable to the people.

Don't believe me? Then ask yourself this question: why has abortion been one of the most polarizing public policy issues of the last forty years? One of the major reasons is because the United States Supreme Court tried to "fix" this problem by legislating from the bench in the 1973 *Roe v. Wade* case.

Soon after Judge John Roberts' confirmation hearings as Chief Justice of the United States in 2005, brilliant and "pro-choice" Charles Krauthammer wrote an extraordinary column that described this very problem:

> In our lifetime has there been a more politically poison-ous Supreme Court decision than Roe v. Wade? Set aside for a moment your thoughts on the substance of the rul-ing. (I happen to be a supporter of legalized abortion.) I'm talking about the continuing damage to the republic: dis-enfranchising, instantly and without recourse, an enor-mous part of the American population; preventing, as even Ruth Bader Ginsburg once said, proper political settlement of the issue by the people and their representa-tives; making us the only nation in the West to have legalized abortion by judicial fiat rather than by the popu-lar will expressed democratically.

Regardless of one's stance on the issue of abortion itself, we need to look at the underlying issue of our judicial system overstepping its bounds, and making decisions at the federal level which should be left to the people in each state. The Court prevented the con-tentious issue of abortion from being debated in each state where elected representatives of their constituents would ultimately reach a consensus. Instead, the issue was removed from the field of legislative deliberation and public hearings, preventing construc-tive give and take, and leaving America with a law that lacks pub-lic acceptance and legitimacy.

I have a consistent pro-life record. I believe that taxpayers should not have to fund abortions. I believe in common sense proposals like parental notification laws and certainly prohibitions against so-called "partial birth abortion." And I believe that the law should reflect our advancement in medical science and knowledge. Thanks to technology like ultrasound, both doctors and parents know much more now about the development and medical "viability" of unborn babies than we did when the Supreme Court ruled on abortion in 1973.

But really, the issue is not whether one is "pro-life" or "pro-choice." We should all be able to agree it is wrong for unelected justices to usurp the rights of voters and legislators and create new laws and new rights simply because that is the will of a majority of the justices themselves.

CALLING BALLS AND STRIKES

I was serving in the United States Senate when President George W. Bush nominated John Roberts for confirmation as Chief Justice of the Supreme Court. I was proud to be one of the U.S. Senators who voted for him (and soon thereafter for Justice Samuel Alito). Roberts, who once played football, invoked a sports referee metaphor to describe his view of a judge's role. As Roberts put it, a Supreme Court Justice is to "call balls and strikes" like an umpire, not "pitch or bat" like a player.

Baseball fanatic and exquisite political columnist George Will likes to use the same image of the judge as umpire. Here's how Will described the parallels in function between baseball umpiring and judicial decision-making in a 2009 column: "Sport—strenuous exertion structured and restrained by rules—replicates the challenges of political freedom. Umpires, baseball's judicial branch, embody what any society always needs and what America, in its current financial disarray, craves—regulated striving that, by preventing ordered competition from descending into chaos, enables excellence to prevail."

George Will marvels at the fact that a baseball hitter who fails two-thirds of the time for fifteen years typically gets named to the Baseball Hall of Fame, yet an umpire "can fail once in a high-stakes moment and be remembered for that forever." Yet, in many ways, the higher standard to which umpires are held in "their pursuit of unobtrusive perfection" is justifiable. This is because our system of government, and our wider society, depend heavily on having an impartial judicial branch that is above reproach and fair in the administration of the rule of law. As author Bruce Weber writes: "As the umpire, you are neither inside the game, as the players are, nor outside it among the fans, but . . . the game passes through you, like rainwater through a filter, and . . . your job is to influence it for the better, to strain out the impurities."

A foundational principle of our Republic, a representative democracy, is that law-making is the function of the elected officials in the legislative and executive branches of government. It is not the role of the judiciary. Just as the NFL's—and all other sports leagues'—rules committee periodically legislates changes to its rules, America's elected officials at the federal, state, and local levels are more than capable of making changes to the laws wanted by the people they represent.

Let's make sure judges are referees, fairly interpreting and administering the law, not inventing it. For as various sports scandals have taught us: when umpires can't be trusted, everyone loses.

CHAPTER NINE

A LOCKER ROOM DIVIDED AGAINST ITSELF CANNOT SURVIVE

WHEN ARMY AND NAVY RENEW THEIR ANNUAL RIVALRY AT the end of every football season, no one is ever quite sure whether the game itself will be the main attraction—or whether the pageantry and pranks surrounding the game will take center stage. Certainly, the Cadets and Midshipmen have played their share of classic gridiron battles.

In 1926, more than 110,000 fans watched an undefeated Navy team led by All-American Frank Wickhorst tie Army 21–21 in the first-ever game played at Soldier Field in Chicago. Among the fans in attendance that day was Notre Dame football coach Knute Rockne, who was so interested in seeing this classic rivalry that he actually skipped his own team's game against Pittsburgh. (In Rockne's absence, Pitt upset the Irish, 19–0.)

In 1944, an undefeated Army team led by "Mr. Inside" Doc Blanchard and "Mr. Outside" Glenn Davis beat Navy 23–7 to complete the Black Knights' perfect season and win Army its first of two consecutive national championships. Blanchard and Davis would each go on to win a Heisman Trophy, and the pair would finish their careers at Army as the only backfield tandem to ever be named All-American three straight years.

In 1963, future Hall of Fame quarterback Roger Staubach led Navy to a 21–15 win over Army in a nationally televised game that featured the first-ever use of instant replay. After Army's first score, CBS commentator Lindsey Nelson had to explain to the viewing audience that they were not watching the Cadets score again. "Ladies and gentlemen, what you are seeing is a tape of Army's touchdown," Nelson said. "This is not live."

In addition to football memories, the Army-Navy game has also had its share of rowdy, raucous, audacious, off-the-field shenanigans.

In 1894, for example, President Grover Cleveland called a special meeting *of his cabinet* to discuss ways to preserve the reputation of the military academies after brawls in the stands and a near-duel between a retired general and a rear admiral marred the 1893 Army-Navy game. President Cleveland cancelled the game indefinitely. Several years later, President William McKinley revived the annual tradition.

In 1953, President Dwight D. Eisenhower, a West Point grad, ordered the Army cadets to return Navy's billy goat mascot to Annapolis after a group of West Point cadets conducted the first of many successful kidnappings of the opposing school's mascot during the week leading up to the big game.

In 1975, Navy alum H. Ross Perot got revenge for his graduating class (1953) when he snuck onto the West Point campus the night before the big game and serenaded the cadets from the chapel belfry with a medley of "Anchors Aweigh," "The Marine Hymn," and "Sailing, Sailing." Perot was captured by some cadets and turned over to military police.

In 2007, an international peace conference being held in Annapolis the week of the big game caused Navy midshipmen to rein in their pranks, doing little beyond the customary effigy-burning of an Army mule at a mid-week pep rally. But the peace conference didn't stop a group of West Point cadets from sneaking onto the Annapolis campus and burning a special message into the Naval Academy's parade field grass. That message read: "Go Army."

So, in addition to some smash-mouth football, the Army-Navy game has also been the impetus for all sorts of good-natured off-the-field fun. More than anything, though, the Army-Navy game has featured moments that remind everyone that even though the service academies very much want to beat each other on the football field, their fierce rivalry is characterized by a profound sense of mutual respect and national solidarity.

During World War II, for example, travel restrictions prevented students at the academies from going to away games. So in 1942, under orders from their superiors, some Navy midshipmen filled the visitors stands in Annapolis and cheered for the Army team. In 1943, some Army cadets returned the favor at West Point. When the travel restrictions were lifted prior to the 1944 game, a fleet of five Navy destroyers escorted a steamer full of Army cadets into Baltimore Harbor to attend the game.

Perhaps no moment, however, can top the scene at the end of every Army-Navy game when the players for both academies gather together to listen to the playing of each other's school songs in a show of mutual appreciation and great sportsmanship.

"Army-Navy is like playing your brother," Navy safety Gary Lane told a *Smithsonian* magazine reporter after the 1999 game. "You play harder, but you share something because you know what the other guy has been through."

"LIKE PLAYING YOUR BROTHER"

The Army-Navy football rivalry should be appreciated because it symbolizes how our national politics should be conducted. In the Army-Navy game, both sides fight hard. They bring creative passion to the competition and desperately want to win. Yet, they never lose sight that they are clashing with "brothers"—with fellow Americans who have pledged to serve their country in the armed services. That very fact helps to foster not only the sense of rivalry between the schools, but the playful atmosphere that surrounds the week of pranks and good-natured needling of the opposition.

I've seen this sort of fierce-but-friendly rivalry first-hand, having grown up around two great rivalries. The first, when I was in grade school, was the historic Chicago Bears-Green Bay Packers rivalry, which would have losing fans swim in the frigid Chicago River. And of course I grew up amidst the storied Redskins-Cowboys NFL rivalry of the 1970s; in fact, many of my fondest memories of my dad's coaching career revolve around that rivalry: like the time my father re-named Redskins player Dallas Hickman "Dulles" Hickman, saying, "From now on your name is Dulles." Or the time my father fired up his players prior to a Dallas game by putting on a Tae Kwon Do and Karate demonstration learned from Grand Master Jhoon Rhee—breaking boards with a side-kick (and nearly breaking his hand with an overly ambitious attempt to karate chop too many stacked boards).

The antics and banter and insults would be put on the locker room walls. A memorable example was remembered by Comcast Sports Net correspondent Rich Tandler, who recounted a 1970s incident, when Redskins' defensive end Ron "Dancing Bear" McDole was asked what he thought about the Dallas quarterback. McDole growled, "Roger Staubach can't read defenses and wears skirts." The more diplomatic Staubach said of McDole and the Redskins: "We don't like them; they don't like us."

I still enjoy the Redskins-Cowboys rivalry in other, more considerate ways. In a demonstration of respect like the Army-Navy rivalry, I first met Dallas Cowboys owner Jerry Jones when he came to Redskins' owner Jack Kent Cooke's funeral. Amazingly to most folks, Jones and I became friends. I'll never forget the gracious hospitality of the Jerry Jones family when I was at their home several years ago for a political fundraiser, attended by Roger Staubach. Jerry was invigorating, and he blew my father's Redskins coaches whistle, which my mother had just given me.

Another treat of the night was seeing Jones's billiard table. His billiard balls don't have traditional "stripes" and "solids"; they feature the colors and helmet logos of the "Redskins" and "Cowboys" instead—with a zebra-striped 8-ball to represent the referees.

These sorts of friendships and new alliances occur often in the world of sports.

Sometimes, players from rivals can join your team by trade or free agency. Examples are Calvin Hill and Duane Thomas coming from the Cowboys, or John Riggins from the Jets, to the Redskins. A more recent example is Brett Favre's circuitous move to the Minnesota Vikings from the rival Green Bay Packers. The Packers' unsuccessful attempt to pay Favre $20 million in 2008 NOT to play football could easily be seen as an imitation of the ludicrous approach of the government to pay farmers NOT to farm. Brett Favre's success in the 2009 season, and especially his two victories over the Packers, were exciting scenes of emotion and justice. And the Easter day acquisition of nemesis Eagle quarterback Donovan McNabb by the Redskins proves that football teams will welcome the best talent available to help their team succeed.

I wish that in our politics we could have the same good nature that we have in our sports rivalries.

To be sure, politics, like sports, aren't for the faint of heart. They aren't tiddlywinks. For without a spirited back-and-forth debate, policies won't be honed and sharpened. The people's business deserves vigorous scrutiny, and differing political philosophies and solutions need to be debated and compete for support. If we're open to actually listening to what the other guy is saying, we can learn something and sometimes even make surprising new allies. I've had this experience.

In 1997, Paul Gillis, a leader of the NAACP in the South Hampton Roads area of Virginia, called for my resignation after I issued an historical proclamation recognizing Virginia's Confederate history. Paul even came to the Old Dominion's traditional bipartisan political event, the Shad Planking among the pine trees of Southeastern Virginia, to tell me so personally. The Shad Planking is one of the best, good-natured political events in Virginia (though sometimes designated drivers are needed). So I was caught by surprise when Paul got right in front of me and started yelling. Several men grabbed him to pull him away, but I told them to let him go and let him have his say. Paul was passionate, and I replied that my intentions were meant to be honorable. After fifteen minutes or so, the tense discussion was over.

Three years later, I was running for the U.S. Senate. Then State Senator (now Congressman) Randy Forbes asked me to meet with

Paul to see if he could be persuaded to support my campaign. Randy insisted that if we discussed our respective views, we'd find we had much in common. So we met.

Paul and I shook hands as we met in Randy and Shirley Forbes's living room. We sat and talked about ideas, philosophy, and goals. After sharing our perspectives for several hours, Paul Gillis and I became political teammates and, though it meant political attacks on him, he campaigned for me. He is a rare man of strong character.

Three years later, in 2003, I was invited to participate in the Civil Rights Pilgrimage in Alabama. As a U.S. Senator, I was allowed to invite one guest; I invited Paul Gillis.

My friend sat next to me as first-hand descriptions of the tactics, operations, and strategies of the Civil Rights movement were explained to those of us assembled. As stated in chapter 1, hearing from the still-living heroes of this just cause during the Pilgrimage had a profound impact on me. And I wish I had learned, fully comprehended, and experienced those lessons years previously, because the harsh, oppressive racial laws were so remote from the integrated football teams my father coached and the world in which I was raised.

One of the seminars in Alabama educated us on the faith-based and especially non-violent aspects of the daunting quest for equal rights. Afterward, I asked Paul if he had been expecting to be physically harmed in that Shad Planking confrontation six years previously. He answered that he had in fact expected to be injured, but he believed sustained injuries might help his claim. He told me he was "willing to get an ass-kicking" to make his point. It really touched my sensibilities, though, to learn that Paul determined the worth of my character in that tense confrontation, when I told my supporters to let him have his say. He had been testing me, and I didn't know it.

There are many lessons to be learned from this story of my friendship with and appreciation of Paul Gillis. For one thing, always be open to the perspective of others. Remember, there is no reason for violence in the advocacy of ideas. And, in some instances, you can recruit new teammates to your own cause just by listening with basic respect.

THE SMART CREDIT

In sports, in life, and in any endeavor, one should always be looking to adapt, innovate, and improve. And one's decisions should be based upon the merits of an idea, not personalities, politics, or process. A prime example of this postulate is my partnering with the energetic Paul Goldman, former Chairman of the Democratic Party of Virginia, on an initiative to modernize as many as one-third of public school buildings in our country that are over fifty years old.

We named our initiative the School Modernization and Revitalization Tax Credit, or SMART Credit.

Together, Paul Goldman (who first approached me with this idea) and I have written op-eds, held press conferences, television interviews, worked with legislative staff on Capitol Hill, and talked to the Richmond Crusade for Voters civil rights organization, contractors, financial leaders, and local, state, and federal officials for this positive, constructive solution to improve opportunities for school children. Most, though not all, old schools in dire need of renovation are in inner cities and rural communities, so the needs are prevalent in communities throughout America.

To renovate an old school, our SMART Credit does not require the federal government to tax, spend, bailout, or borrow a nickel. A simple one-sentence change to the federal "historic tax credit" law would allow the 20 percent federal tax credit to be used by local schools for historic school renovation by private investors. By removing the "prior use" impediment, billions of private sector dollars will be available for school renovation.

Our SMART Credit achieves four important goals. First, school children will be learning in modernized school facilities. A quality facility does not ensure success, but dilapidated facilities make academic success very difficult for students and teachers. Second, jobs would be created in building, construction, and supplies (a multiplier effect) for all the electricians, masons, carpenters, and suppliers involved in the renovation project. Third, taxpayers would save money by spending at least 20 percent less on school construction. Where additional state tax credits are available, revitalizing our schools with SMART would save taxpayers 30 percent over traditional funding means, as well as preserving the heritage of older school buildings. And fourth, new, modernized schools would be more energy efficient with better systems that will require less energy to heat, cool, illuminate, and operate the buildings. Lower operating costs save taxpayers additional money during the extended life of the school.

Since introducing this idea, it has been supported by a diverse coalition, from Terry McAuliffe (former Chairman of the Democratic National Committee), both Democratic and Republican Members of Congress, and both Candidates in the 2009 race for Virginia Governor: Creigh Deeds and my good friend Bob McDonnell, who said: "This idea, to allow private investors to modernize an old school, and then lease it back to school districts for use, is one that I strongly support. Governor Allen and Paul Goldman deserve our thanks for advancing this positive solution."

People on different sides of the political aisle can lose sight of the fact that we all ultimately play for Team America. There is always more that should unite us than divide us. Our common goal should always be what's best for the people we serve.

I know that in the heat of political competition I've said things that were meant to be political banter—but the equivalent of sports-like exhortations are better left on the field. One that I concocted in a locker room before addressing the Republican Party of Virginia's 1994 Convention didn't work as intended. The over 10,000 Convention Delegates nominating Ollie North for Senate cheered at my closing charge, "My friends, and I say this figuratively, let's enjoy knocking their soft teeth down their whiny throats." Rather than thinking of what my father might say to his team in the locker room before a contest, I should have considered that it was far from the right way to address a political gathering. I should have listened to the sound advice of such trusted people as my wife Susan and my Chief of Staff Jay Timmons, who counseled me against using such a line.

I was reminded of this difference in reading Gregg Rosenthal's January 13, 2010, NBCSports.com blog post on Coach Joe Bugel's retirement press conference, in which he talked about football players who "knock the snot right outta yer head" and said "I don't have a big vocabulary, but I know every swear word." Rosenthal reports that the "writers in attendance were ready to block for the man." That is as big a difference between sports and politics, as I have learned over the years.

I made another mistake—a much more painful one for everyone involved—in a clumsy attempt to tweak my opponent on the campaign trail during my re-election campaign for the United States Senate in 2006. My opponent had a cameraman who followed me to dozens of public events on my annual Listening Tour throughout Virginia. This young man was simply doing his videotaping job—a difficult one at that. While we were campaigning all over Virginia, my opponent was reportedly out in "surreal" Hollywood. It was my intention to chide him, through his staffer's camera, by welcoming my opponent to the "real world" of Virginia, where people had real world concerns related to jobs and opportunities. In the process I gave the young cameraman the unfortunate, made-up nickname of Macaca(or Makaka). I thought of it as a nonsense word. If I had known the nickname could be considered a racial slur, I would not have said it. But that was how it was characterized. The poor judgment was mine. I should never have dragged this young man into the debate when my real target was my opponent. I apologized to him, and take full responsibility for the remark and its aftermath, which should have been handled much better.

I regret my words, I regret how they were misdirected, I regret how I let down our hardworking team, and I regret that a campaign I had hoped would be focused on ideas and my record in the Senate devolved into a media frenzy focused on word origins, insults, and a game of gotcha politics.

Beyond the campaign, it was particularly heart-wrenching and painful to let down my whole family, who had to endure taunts and insults because of my action. I know first hand the toll that political life can take on family members. This incident and the ensuing frenzy made life even more agonizing for my family. And, personally, it hurt to watch my opposition mischaracterize my record and the person I am.

Politics has always been a contact sport, and even our Founding Fathers didn't see eye to eye. Yet, in the end, they pledged to each other—and to America's grand experiment in self-government—"our lives, our fortunes, and our sacred honor." As familiar as that phrase is, it is important for us to remember what united the founders. Their genius did not lie in getting along despite their differences, but in fashioning a system of self-government that guarded personal liberty and ensured equal justice. As the son of an immigrant mother who came to America after her home was liberated from the Nazis by Allied Forces in World War II, I passionately believe liberty and justice should be the goals of all of us in political life. We might have different ideas of how to achieve these goals. But we need to always remember that these are our common American ideals; and in serving them we should listen to each other, afford each other respect, and then play hard for the political team that best represents what we think to be right way to achieve those goals.

LOCKER ROOM DIVISIONS

Few truths are illustrated in sports better than this one. For as anyone who has ever been in a sports locker room knows, much of the success of a team on the field depends on how well the players identify with one another off the field.

We know the pages of sports history books are filled with stories of better-talented teams that came up short in crucial games because they were torn by internal dissension—and with stories of scrappy underdogs that pulled off "miraculous" big-game upset victories because they played together as a cohesive unit.

Throughout my life, I saw how my father emphasized team unity; he would emphasize to all his players assembled on the sidelines before a game that "40 men working together can't lose." He reminded them that they would rise or fall as one, as a team.

His players adhered to this team concept, even (or perhaps especially) when it was tested in defeat. "Some week we'll go out and get our butts blown off, but no one will start pointing fingers," Redskins wide receiver Charley Taylor once told a reporter. "We have a family here like no other team in the league has." This was a family that extended to my mother and sister Jennifer with the players' and coaches' families. Whether cheering from the stands or on the side-lines, everyone was a member of the Redskins family.

The concept of a team rising or falling as one reminds us of the deep rift on the Dallas Cowboys between "Team Romo" (those loyal to quarterback Tony Romo) and "Team T. O." (those loyal to wide receiver Terrell Owens). At the time, legendary coach Bill Parcells was at the Cowboys' helm. And in an attempt to get every-one on the same page, Parcells posted some signs around the Dallas Cowboys locker room. One read, "Losers assemble in little groups and bitch about the coaches and the system and other players in other little groups. Winners assemble as a team."

Parcell's disdain for people who foment dissension rather than confronting problems in an above-board manner is a message politicians in Washington need to hear. For with the rise of insular internet networks that serve as "echo chambers" for certain politi-cal viewpoints, our political culture today has a lot of whiners, complainers, and other aggrieved parties who can find a sympa-thetic ear very easily. And this, in turn, can prompt some in our day to feign offense at the drop of a hat (like those "floppers" on the soccer field who try to coax the referee into calling a penalty against their opponent by pretending to be the victim of some hor-rendous violation).

Representative democracy isn't always pretty. Naturally, imperfect people will often act imperfectly. And just as we need a system of government with many "checks and balances" to pro-tect us from the tyrannical tendencies of imperfect people, we also need people in that system who are prepared to deal, seri-ously, maturely, and wisely, with challenges affecting the people of our nation. We need people on both sides of the aisle who will confront differences directly, who will help us to find unity around founding principles, and who will overlook personal slights and foolish chatter with common sense, thick skin, and a sense of humor.

"KILMERESQUE" GUSTO

Since involuntarily leaving the Senate in 2007, I have continued to learn and strive to improve. It is certainly true that in times like these, one finds who his real friends are. Many people have encouraged me to run for public office again. My answer is "perhaps." As long as I'm breathing, I'll be advocating for ways to revive our economy, create new jobs, improve our education system, slash wasteful government spending (as Chairman of the American Energy Freedom Center and Reagan Ranch Presidential Scholar for the Young America's Foundation), and achieve strategic energy independence. I'll also be doing everything I can to help candidates who reflect the common sense conservatism I believe in. Many people have helped me though the years—people like Congressman J. Kenneth Robinson, Senator John Warner, Lawrence Eagleburger, Jack Kemp, Cap Weinberger, and thousands of good friends like Bob and Suzy Pence, Walter Curt, Lawrence Lewis, Hunter and Carl Smith, Bessie Birckhead, Ron Robinson, and John and Becky Matney—and I want to do for other candidates what these especially kind people did for me: provide counsel and support. While not closing any doors, I know this—whatever I do, I want to do with "Kilmeresque" gusto.

If that sounds like a strange statement, let me explain.

Over the course of my father's long career in coaching, few players personified his most prized ideals in a football player more than quarterback Billy Kilmer. Admittedly, Kilmer was hardly a "choir boy." In fact, he had many nicknames on the Redskins, including "Whiskey" and "Furnace Face." And on two different occasions, Kilmer's pro football career almost came to an abrupt end because of his poor judgment off the field.

Still, Billy Kilmer distinguished himself as a gritty, cut-nose player who learned from his mistakes and never, ever, ever gave up. He was a fighter who had the heart of a champion. That's why Kilmer was loved so much by his fellow players and coaches—and why his example is so inspiring.

Kilmer's first "self-inflicted wound" occurred in the early 1960s, when he was playing for the San Francisco 49ers after starring at UCLA. The story is that one day Kilmer fell asleep at the wheel and drove his car off the Bayshore Freeway and into San Francisco Bay. Billy was lucky to have lived through this wreck, much less play football again. He suffered a serious and permanent leg injury in the accident which prevented him from playing football the following season and relegated him to a back-up role for several seasons after that.

Forced to re-tool his game and become more of a passer than a runner, Kilmer kept adapting and fighting. The 49ers deemed Kilmer expendable, and he eventually landed with the expansion New Orleans Saints, where he started at quarterback for four brutal seasons. In 1971, the Saints drafted my high school idol, the heroic Archie Manning, and Billy Kilmer was once again an "expendable" back up. Then, soon after being named head coach of the Washington Redskins, my father traded a fourth round draft choice and a backup linebacker for Kilmer.

With the Redskins, Kilmer was known for throwing wobbly passes; but his "wounded ducks" managed to get the job done when the exquisitely perfect spiral-passing Sonny Jurgensen got injured. And with Kilmer at the helm, the Redskins achieved their first appearance in the playoffs in more than a quarter-century by winning their memorable Monday Night Football regular season finale against the Rams, a game that was watched by 66 million viewers.

One reason so many people tuned in to see that game was because Kilmer had been in the headlines all week, following his arrest for "disorderly conduct" in the wee hours of the night, after Washington had won its previous game. Refusing to let this embarrassing incident hinder his team's quest for the playoffs, Kilmer went out and threw for 246 yards and 3 touchdowns to lead the Redskins to a 38–24 playoff-clinching victory in the L.A. Coliseum— a win my dad at the time called "the best win of our lives."

So, Billy Kilmer had feet of clay. He made some mistakes in his life. But he got up and came back fighting every time. And in the course of persevering through his adversities, Kilmer once managed to perform a feat that I suspect all of us would like to be able to orchestrate somehow in our personal lives: Billy once fumbled, yet his turnover led to points for his team.

It is, in fact, one of the most famous plays in NFL history. It took place while Kilmer was playing for the 49ers in a 1964 game against the Minnesota Vikings. Kilmer caught a pass from the team's starting quarterback, and after advancing the ball several yards up the field, he was hit, fumbled, and then watched as Minnesota defensive lineman Jim Marshall scooped up the ball and ran all the way to the end zone. The Vikings' end zone.

Jim Marshall's wrong-way run gave a safety point to the 49ers. The Vikings still won the game, and Marshall went on to set the all-time NFL record for most fumble recoveries in a career. But this embarrassing moment teaches an important lesson: that you never know how a fumble might turn out. Most people remember Marshall's mistake, of how a good play (a fumble recovery) can go terribly wrong (just as a good deed can blow up in our faces). But I'm convinced that we really ought to focus at least as much attention on Kilmer's unusual good fortune. What looked like a disaster turned out not to be.

What I learned from Billy Kilmer is that while we all make mistakes, we can't let those mistakes make us gun shy, or afraid to take risks, or lead us to sit back and be a critic rather than a participant. We need to go out and play hard every day. In a phrase: I believe in living with "Kilmeresque gusto." Because we're not perfect, "self-inflicted wounds" are almost inevitable. But the optimistic, overcoming, fighting spirit that Kilmer displayed on the football field also holds out this possibility: even when you fumble, you might be able to score points; and you certainly can't score points unless you're in the game and willing to take risks.

Each of us is put here on earth to do something well. We cheat ourselves and we cheat others when we don't use our unique talents to our full potential.

KEEP FIGHTING

There are infinitesimally rare "perfect" games in sports or life. When I was unfairly "redistricted" out of a House of Representatives seat that I had just won in a special election, people encouraged—and convinced—me to run for Governor of Virginia.

Our "insurgent" campaign won a hotly contested intrasquad scrimmage-nomination contest. After winning the nomination, my fellow Republican contestants, Earle Williams and Delegate Clint Miller, supported my candidacy. But in early June our campaign was out of money, and we were over four touchdowns (thirty-one points) behind well-funded, two-time Attorney General Mary Sue Terry. We had, however, audacious ideas for improving our criminal justice system and public safety, bettering education, reforming welfare and government spending, and encouraging businesses to create more job opportunities in Virginia.

For inspiration, I sent copies of my father's "Keep Fighting" poster to our growing "A-Team." It was written by my dad when he was chairman of President Reagan's Council on Physical Fitness and Sports. (The poster has been reproduced in Appendix A.)

We worked hard to get our message of hope and reform to the people of Virginia, and the voters responded and agreed with our ideas and transformational proposals. We ultimately won a three-way race with 58 percent of the vote because of the grassroots support of people who saw that our agenda would make Virginia a better place to live, learn, work, invest, and raise our families. It was a great come-from-behind victory for our campaign and our band of insurgents. We won because we motivated, inspired, and united Virginians for our initiatives and right policies, and because we kept fighting.

No matter what the odds, never give up. After I lost reelection to the U.S. Senate in 2006 by less than an extra point, I knew the lesson remained the same. When you get knocked down, you have to get back up; learn from your mistakes and improve. So long as they don't kill you, you can keep fighting for your beliefs and ideals.

"THE MAN IN THE ARENA"

The notion that you can't make a difference unless you're in the game is consistent with a speech Teddy Roosevelt gave in 1910 at the Sorbonne in Paris. Roosevelt said this:

> It is not the critic who counts; not the man who points out how the strong man stumbles, or where the doer of deeds could have done them better.

The credit belongs to the man who is actually in the arena, whose face is marred by dust and sweat and blood; who strives valiantly; who errs, who comes short again and again, because there is no effort without error and short-coming; but who does actually strive to do the deeds; who knows great enthusiasms, the great devotions; who spends himself in a worthy cause; who at the best knows in the end the triumph of high achievement, and who at the worst, if he fails, at least fails while daring greatly, so that his place shall never be with those cold and timid souls who neither know victory nor defeat.

Like Teddy Roosevelt—like Billy Kilmer—our place should not be "with those cold and timid souls who neither know victory nor defeat." Wherever we're called to serve, we should do so as "happy warriors." As a nation we must reject complacency; we must never accept decline. Our goal should always be to improve ourselves, our community, our states, our nation. Our America must always be that beacon of hope and freedom, that Shining City on a Hill that we all know and love.

Surely, our nation today has many challenges that demand strong leadership; and, as I've sought to describe in this book, many of our problems could be better solved if lawmakers learned some lessons from sports, including the importance of equal opportunity; fair competition (on a level playing field); and having judges who are impartial umpires, not players. They could learn the urgent importance of having a strong defense and energy security. And they could learn a lot about teamwork, perseverance, accountability, leadership, and discipline, which are characteristic of the competitive meritocracy of sports.

Sports can be a great teacher in the larger pursuits of life. When the Duke of Wellington, Arthur Wellesley, was asked how England had defeated Napoleon, he replied: "The Battle of Waterloo was won on the [rugby] playing fields of Eton." With equal justice, one could say that the United States won the battle of Midway on the football fields of Annapolis and Texas high schools, the stickball streets of Brooklyn, the boxing rings of Los Angeles, and the basketball courts of Chicago.

Today, America is engaged in a great war against global terrorism. We are trying to get out from under a deep and painful recession while competing with people from larger countries to produce more innovative goods and services. We are challenged to create a better, more wholesome America for our children. There are plenty of challenges for our nation's leaders. I hope they learn some of the lessons of this book. And I hope and pray that, whatever the challenges, we will choose to stand strong for freedom. In order for justice and liberty to prevail and endure, however intense the political debate, we all must remember that we are part of Team America—we are all Americans first.

J. C. WATTS

In the late 1970s I made a small splash as quarterback of the University of Oklahoma's football team, acting as field general for Barry Switzer's wishbone offense. In junior high and high school I played football, baseball, and basketball, and I boxed for three years. I owe much of my never say die spirit to what I learned in athletics and especially football.

George Allen in this wonderful book, *What Washington Can Learn from the World of Sports*, articulates so well what sports capture and create in the psyche of men and women. Sports encourage red, yellow, brown, black, and white to ignore skin color, ignore economic background, ignore single family backgrounds, and focus on a common goal. Sports teach how to succeed through hard work, common effort, and clear standards. When I stepped on the football field, or the basketball court, or the baseball diamond, or into the boxing ring, I knew the rules were the same for me and my opponent.

I've enjoyed success in sports, business, and politics, and I can tell you that sports were the easiest field to navigate because the rules were clear—and we'd be a lot better off, as George Allen points out, if the principles we apply in athletics were applied in all walks of life and most especially in politics. In Washington they often think they know all the answers, but they'd be well advised to read this book and apply its excellent common sense to the issues that confront our nation.

—J. C. Watts played professional football, is an ordained Baptist minister, and served four terms as a United States Congressman from Oklahoma

ACKNOWLEDGEMENTS

There were many key players in the composition of this book. As in any significant endeavor, one needs trusted teammates.

Thank you to the MVP, Bill Mattox, for his dedicated, essential, and patient friendship, and his adaptive creativity. There is no one I've ever met who has as much thoughtful, detailed, and enthusiastic knowledge of sports as well as a passion for political theory. Bill's outstanding work on the sports stories I've retold is greatly appreciated. His assistance was invaluable in helping me write this book, which my wife Susan and others had encouraged me to write for many years.

The love of my life, Susan—"Chicory"—is the best coach and teammate one could enjoy. It is with Susan's encouragement that I have written this book. It was fate, and an absentee ballot, that brought us together many years ago. It is with her devotion, dedication, and partnership that we have served the people of Virginia together while maintaining the tough balance between public service and raising three wonderful children: Tyler, Forrest, and Brooke. So often in a political family, as in a football family, a good spouse is the glue that holds us all together. For her steadiness and loving leadership, I am forever grateful.

The two greatest influences on me were my parents: my father, who immersed me in his competitive, energetic world of football, and my mother, who is a truly remarkable woman. She experienced the terrifying Axis-occupation of her home country of Tunisia during World War II. As a young girl, the Nazis broke into her home in the dark of night and took her father (my grandfather) away to an unknown place. She survived, as did her whole family including her father, thanks to Tunisia's liberation by American and British troops. Our whole family will always appreciate all the Allied troops who fought in World War II, and in particular those who fought in the North African Theatre.

A few years after the War, my mother went to Sioux City, Iowa, where fortunately, she met my father. They fell in love, got married, and started their family. My father always said his wife Etty was the "clutch" player for our Allen family team.

Growing up, "family" was the one constant in a life of ups and downs, hiring and firings, and moving. My siblings and I continue to share a closeness—and they helped me in this project. In composing this book, I am particularly grateful to my archivist brother Bruce, who has been a leader with the Raiders, Buccaneers, and now the Redskins. He provided me with relevant articles, stories, and photos. My sister Jennifer, an accomplished writer and reporter for the NFL Network, was also an enormous help in finding the photographs for this book. My reverent brother Greg, who does salutary work with young people in Freedom4-U, has been a source of constant prayer and support. My brothers and sister and their spouses and children carry on the Allen family tradition of maintaining the Four F's of life: Faith, Family, Freedom, and Football—not necessarily in that order.

The concept and importance of Faith was inculcated into our lives with "grace" before supper and in all the teams my father coached. Indeed, Tom Skinner, the Redskins' chaplain, remains the best preacher I have ever heard. Tom Skinner meant so much to our family that he officiated my father's funeral. When I was "sworn in" as Governor of Virginia, it was Tom Skinner who provided the passionate invocation.

The concept of Freedom was impressed into us by my mother. In her own way, she would teach us about the blessings of Freedom. And, in times when we were moping about lost games, firings, or other times of stress, my mother would always put it in perspective: "At least there are no bombs falling on us."

Throughout my years of public service and in the private sector, there have been many teammates who influenced me and helped me. I greatly appreciate the crucial, loyal, spirited assistance of the leaders and insurgents of our A-Team. Some of these A-Team leaders were helpful in writing this book, including Jay Timmons, Kay Coles James, Dan "Crawfish" Allen, Frank Atkinson, "Heavens to Betsy" Beamer, Mike Thomas, Becky Norton Dunlop, Rob Martinez, Johnny Mazza, Sandy Liddy Bourne, Paul Gillis, Tim Nussbaum, and Henry "King of the Road" Doggett.

To compete and succeed in the worlds of politics and sports, one needs great teammates, encouraging supporters, and solid coaches. I have been blessed to have had thousands of political supporters, from the "Original Gang," to the "A-Team," to the "insurgents," to the "Ranch and Cow Bosses," as well as football and rugby teammates and coaches, insightful business leaders, dedicated teachers, and wise trainers, all of whom have enriched my life. In and out of public service, I have been blessed with principled, loyal friends. I'm grateful for having the opportunity to personally thank a few of them here. I hope this book will serve as a token of my appreciation for all they've done, and I hope it will provide inspiration to many other Americans to stand strong for freedom.

KEEP FIGHTING

KEEP FIGHTING

One of the most difficult things everyone has to learn is that for your entire life you must "keep fighting" and adjusting if you hope to survive.

Every day is a fight of some type. Some are pleasant, others are not. No matter who you are or what your position, you must "keep fighting" for whatever you desire to achieve.

It doesn't seem right and it doesn't seem fair, but this is the way life is. It is a constant struggle of fighting within yourself to be physically fit and strong when you take on the battle of life.

If someone is not aware of this contest and expects otherwise, then constant disappointment occurs. People who fail sometimes do not realize that the simple answer to everyday achievement is to keep fighting.

It's challenging and exciting. The tougher the job the greater the reward, but winners are in shape and keep fighting. Losers don't know why they are losing.

It's strange, but health, happiness and success depends upon the **fighting spirit** of each person.

The big thing is not what happens to us in life--but what we DO about what happens to us.

Work hard and watch the good things happen!

George H. Allen

by **George H. Allen**
Chairman, President's Council
on Physical Fitness & Sports

Provided as a Public Service by
Atlas Van Lines, Inc. Evansville, IN

APPENDIX B

CONSISTENCY

CONSISTENCY

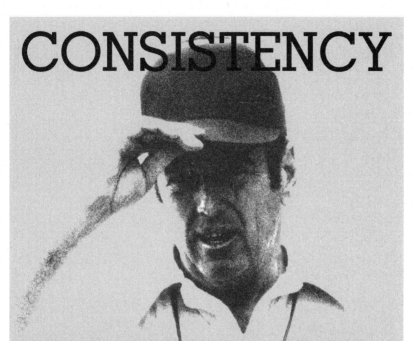

Consistency is the truest measure of performance. Almost anyone can have a great day, or even a good year, but true success is the ability to perform day in and day out, year after year, under all kinds of conditions. Inconsistency will win *some* of the time; consistency will win *most* of the time.

   Consistency requires concentration, determination, and repetition. To be at your best all the time, you must:

   • **Take nothing for granted.** If you are "up" every day, something, or someone, will knock you down.

   • **Take pride in what you do.** The things you do well are the things you enjoy doing.

   • **Take setbacks in stride.** Don't brood over reverses; learn from them.

   • **Take calculated chances.** To win something, you must risk something.

   • **Take work home.** To get ahead, plan ahead.

   • **Take the extra lap.** Condition yourself for the long run. The tested can always take it.

   • **Don't take "no" for an answer.** You can do what you believe you can do.

P.S. – Celebrate _after_ victory!

George H. Allen

George H. Allen
Chairman, President's Council
on Physical Fitness & Sports

INDEX